BECOME AN
APP INVENTOR

THE OFFICIAL GUIDE FROM MIT APP INVENTOR

Your Guide to Designing, Building, and Sharing Apps

The MIT Press, the ☰MITeenPress colophon, and MITeen are trademarks of Massachusetts Institute of Technology and used under license from The MIT Press. The colophon and MITeen are registered in the US Patent and Trademark Office.

First edition 2022

Library of Congress Catalog Card Number 2021939777
ISBN 978-1-5362-1914-2 (hardcover)
ISBN 978-1-5362-2408-5 (paperback)

APS 26 25 24 23 22 21
10 9 8 7 6 5 4 3 2 1

Printed in Humen, Dongguan, China

This book was typeset in Avenir Next.

MITeen Press
an imprint of Candlewick Press
99 Dover Street
Somerville, Massachusetts 02144

miteenpress.com
candlewick.com

BECOME AN
APP INVENTOR

THE OFFICIAL GUIDE FROM MIT APP INVENTOR

Your Guide to Designing, Building, and Sharing Apps

KAREN LANG AND SELIM TEZEL

MIT APP INVENTOR PROJECT

MIT COMPUTER SCIENCE AND ARTIFICIAL INTELLIGENCE LABORATORY

MiTeen Press

CONTENTS

FOREWORD

Developing solutions is fun, especially when the solution involves a mobile application. However, developing mobile applications used to require special programming skills and time. All of that changed for me when I first started using MIT App Inventor. It allowed me to focus on solving a problem rather than spending time on complex code. I wish I'd had this book when I first started playing with App Inventor. With easy instructions that take readers from downloading the MIT AI2 Companion application to creating their own chat app, this book is a beneficial friend for all the young changemakers who have ideas but don't know where to start or don't have a teacher or expert to guide them. Recently, I was contacted by a girl who had an idea for creating an app for dyslexic students like her but did not know how to start or code. I recommended that she use MIT App Inventor. This book is an ideal companion for anybody like her who is passionate about developing mobile apps.

The book starts with simple apps, and each chapter is organized to build on the one before and help readers create progressively more interesting apps. My brother struggled to make a weather app as part of a school assignment. After spending just a few minutes exploring App Inventor and reading through the first chapter, he soon had a prototype ready to go. The book not only allows anybody to build apps relatively quickly, but it also enables teachers and educators to introduce their students to easy mobile app development without having to develop advanced skills themselves. Given that App Inventor allows more time to focus on problem-solving, teachers and educators can now include this in their curriculums for a problem-based learning approach.

Each chapter also features heartwarming true stories of young innovators and changemakers who used App Inventor to solve problems. It was great to read about their journeys from vision to implementation, all using the varied features App Inventor provides.

As a prolific user of MIT App Inventor, I strongly recommend this book for anybody looking to develop mobile apps using MIT App Inventor. I want to thank the authors, Ms. Lang and Mr. Tezel, for providing a step-by-step guide for all young students. This book should be in every library, school, and STEM and coding club, and I hope it will inspire a new generation of inventors and innovators.

Gitanjali Rao
Time magazine's 2020 Kid of the Year

INTRODUCTION

Have you ever played a game on a tablet or watched a video on your phone? If so, you probably used an app to do it. **Mobile applications**, or **apps** for short, are programs designed for use on a device like a phone or tablet. Apps can help you check the weather, look up information online, and share photos with friends.

But where do apps come from? They're built by people called **programmers**. Programmers create a set of instructions that tells a device what to do. They write the instructions in a special language, called a **programming language**, so a computer can understand it. The instructions are also known as **code**, and another name for programmers is **coders**.

// NOTE

A **computer** is a machine that can follow a set of instructions. Computers come in all shapes and sizes. Desktop computers, laptops, tablets, smartphones, smartwatches, security systems, and many car engines and refrigerators are examples of computers. The instructions they follow are called **programs**, and programs that run on mobile devices like phones and tablets are often called apps.

MIT App Inventor is a kind of programming language that uses blocks, which look like puzzle pieces with words on them. The blocks fit together to make instructions that get translated into computer language so a mobile device can follow them.

App Inventor blocks

If you're looking for some App Inventor inspiration, meet Gitanjali Rao, a teen from Lone Tree, Colorado, who was named *Time* magazine's first-ever Kid of the Year in 2020. She's an amazing scientist and innovator and an accomplished app inventor. In 2017, she demonstrated her invention Tethys, which measures lead levels in water. She was inspired to create Tethys by the Flint, Michigan, water crisis, in which the city's drinking water was highly contaminated by lead and was poisoning children. Her device uses carbon nanotubes to detect lead levels and report that information through Bluetooth to an app she created with MIT App Inventor. Since then, Gitanjali has continued to learn and invent. Her latest project is Kindly, an app that helps prevent cyberbullying. The app detects words associated with bullying, notifies the user, and gives them the opportunity to edit their language.

Gitanjali believes that innovation happens when you're inspired and motivated to create something meaningful. Hoping to encourage others, Gitanjali offers innovation workshops to share her knowledge and scientific method with other young people around the globe. She has already mentored thirty thousand kids through her workshops.

What about you? Do you have something that you are passionate about? Does that passion lead you to ideas for new apps? Or maybe you have thoughts about ways to improve an app that already exists. Awesome! This book will teach you how to use MIT App Inventor to take your ideas and turn them into apps for your phone or tablet. Soon you'll be able to share your apps with friends and family and even publish them for people around the world to download and use. Soon you'll be an app inventor too.

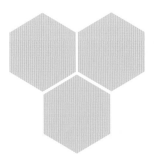

CHAPTER 1

Let's Get Started

There are a few steps you'll need to take before you can dig in and start writing apps. First, you'll need a computer or laptop on which to design and write the code for your apps. Then you'll want to try out your apps with a mobile device. To do that, you'll need to install an app called the MIT AI2 Companion on your phone or tablet so you can load your projects onto your device and test them.

If you're using an Android device, open the Play Store app and search for MIT AI2 Companion. You can also type this link into a browser (like Google Chrome): http://appinv.us/ai-Android. If you are using an iOS device, open the App Store app and search for MIT AI2 companion. You can also use the link http://appinv.us/ai-iOS. Click the button to install the MIT AI2 Companion on your device. The icon for the app will show the mascot, Codi the Bee.

You'll need to install the MIT AI2 Companion only once and then leave it on your phone or tablet for whenever you use App Inventor.

Android users: If you choose not to go through the Play Store and instead load the app directly by using the website link (aka "side load"), you will need to change your device's settings to allow it to install apps from "unknown sources." To find this setting on versions of Android before 4.0, go to Settings > Applications and check the box next to Unknown Sources. For devices running Android 4.0 or above, go to Settings > Security or Settings > Security & Screen Lock and check the box next to Unknown Sources and confirm your choice.

If you don't have access to a mobile device, or don't have a good Wi-Fi connection, there are other ways to test your apps. If you don't have a mobile device, you can use the emulator that App Inventor provides, which looks like a phone but runs in your computer's browser. You can also create and test App Inventor projects with a Chromebook. If Wi-Fi is an issue, you can connect a mobile device to your computer with a USB cable. To get instructions for these other options, open the AI2 Getting Started page (http://bit.ly/ai2-getstarted) in a web browser and click on the instructions for the option you'd like to use.

Once you have set up your mobile device, open a browser like Google Chrome or Mozilla Firefox on your computer.

Logging in with a Gmail Account

If you have a Gmail account, type this address into the URL field: http://ai2.appinventor.mit.edu.

Now all the projects you create will be saved under your account.

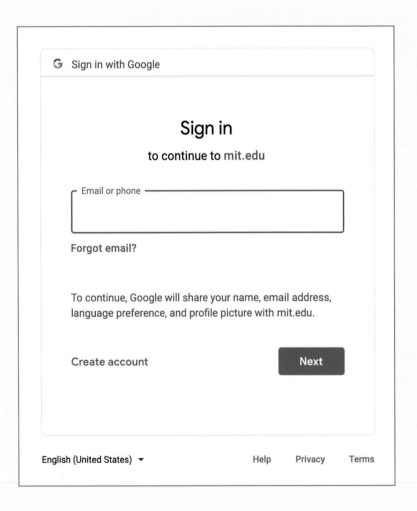

Logging in without a Gmail Account

If you don't have a Gmail account and can't make one, use this address: http://code .appinventor.mit.edu. Just press the button (Continue Without An Account), and you can log on to the server.

Once you press the button, you'll be given a revisit code, which will help you save your projects.

Make sure to copy the revisit code and keep it somewhere safe, because without it, you won't be able to get your projects back! The next time you log in to http://code.appinventor.mit.edu, you will type in your code rather than clicking (Continue Without An Account).

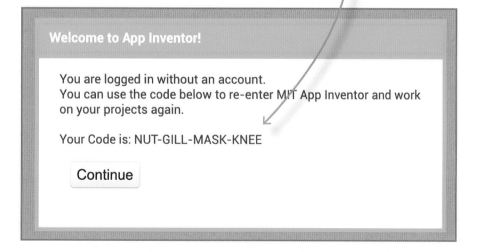

Once You're Logged In

When you log in, you'll see a screen with the latest information about MIT App Inventor and a link to setup instructions. Press the (Continue) button.

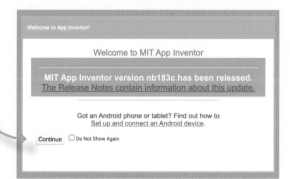

On the next display, which has links to some starter tutorials, press the button on the bottom left labeled (Start a Blank Project).

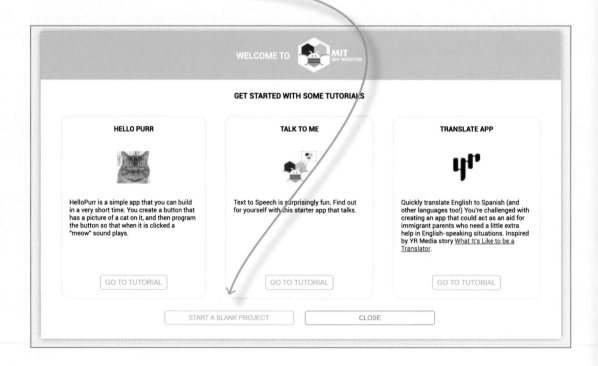

You'll be asked to name your new project. For your first app, you can name it HelloItsMe.

Click (OK). You will see your blank project in the App Inventor IDE. **IDE** stands for interactive development environment, and it's what you'll use to make your apps.

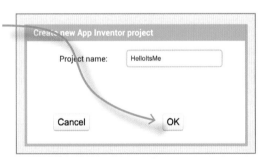

Create new App Inventor project

Project name: HelloItsMe

Cancel   OK

The Designer

Palette

choose and add components

Viewer

arrange components

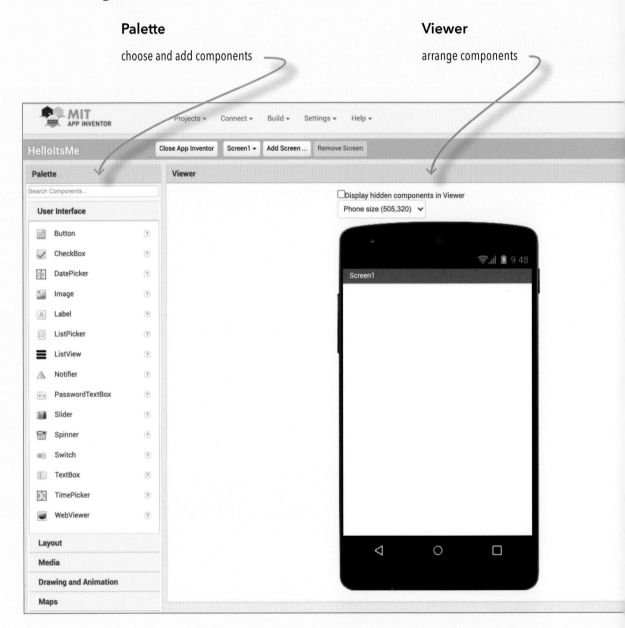

Components

list added components

Properties

change component settings

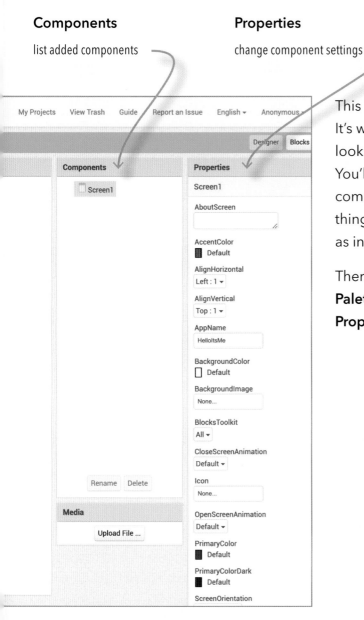

This IDE window is called the **Designer**. It's where you'll decide how your apps look and how users will interact with them. You'll do this by adding and arranging components. **Components** include visible things like buttons and text boxes, as well as invisible things like sounds and sensors.

There are four panels in the Designer: **Palette**, **Viewer**, **Components**, and **Properties**.

The Palette Panel

On the left in the Designer is the Palette. The Palette lists all the components you can add to your app, organized in drawers according to their type. If you click on a drawer, it will expand so you can see the components inside.

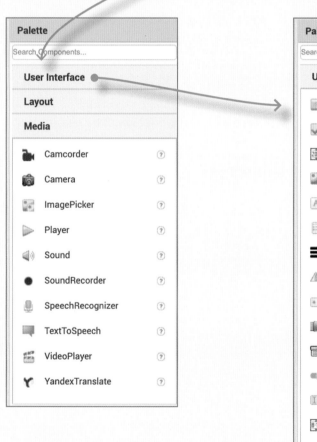

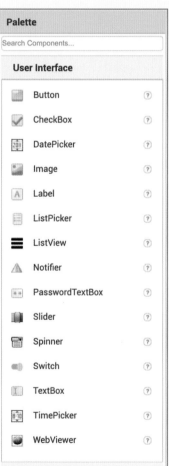

The Viewer Panel

To select a component, click on it, drag it, and drop it onto the phone screen image that appears in the second panel, the Viewer.

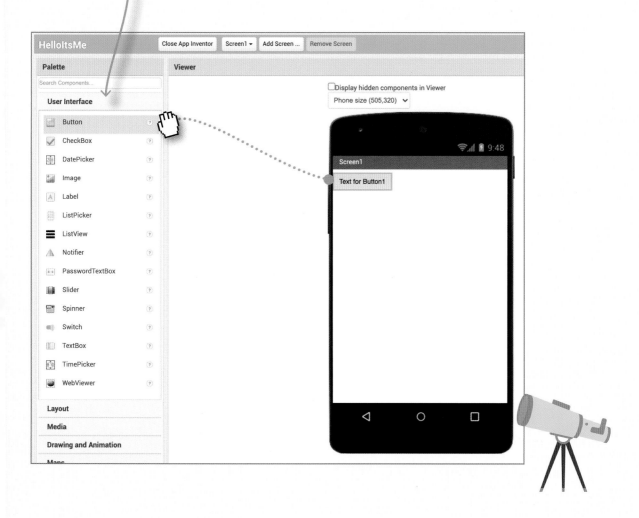

The Components Panel

As you drag components to the Viewer to add them to your app, they also appear in a list in the Components panel.

The Properties Panel

You can select a component by clicking on it in the Viewer or in the Components panel. Once a component is selected, you can change its settings in the Properties panel.

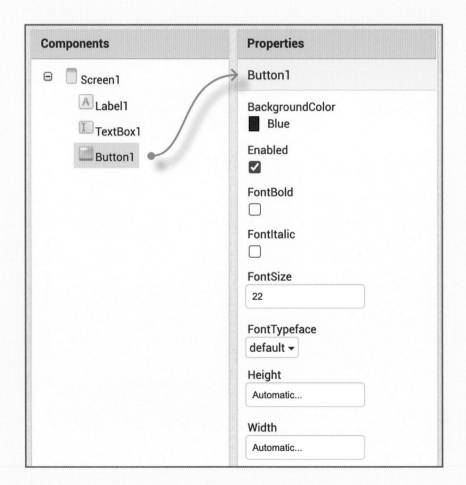

For example, if you select **Button1**, you can make changes to things like its background color, font size, shape, text, and text color!

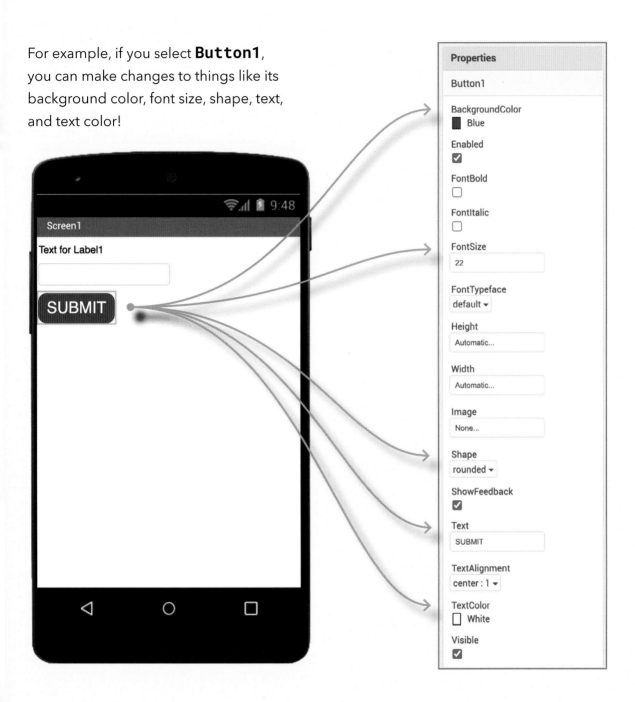

Properties

Button1

BackgroundColor
■ Blue

Enabled
☑

FontBold
☐

FontItalic
☐

FontSize
22

FontTypeface
default ▾

Height
Automatic...

Width
Automatic...

Image
None...

Shape
rounded ▾

ShowFeedback
☑

Text
SUBMIT

TextAlignment
center : 1 ▾

TextColor
☐ White

Visible
☑

The Blocks Editor

Once you've added your components in the Designer, you can switch to the **Blocks Editor** by clicking on the (Blocks) button in the upper-right corner.

In the Blocks Editor, instead of dragging components the way you do in the Designer, you'll drag out various code blocks that fit together like puzzle pieces. These blocks are the instructions that tell your app what to do. The main difference between the Designer and the Blocks Editor is that the Designer controls the look and feel of your app, whereas the Blocks Editor controls the behavior of your app. You'll need them both to build a successful app.

The Blocks Palette

On the left in the Blocks Editor is the **Blocks** palette. This is where you can find all the blocks, divided into two sections—**Built-in** blocks and **Component** blocks.

Built-in Blocks

Built-in blocks are organized by category. Clicking on the category makes its blocks appear. For example, clicking on Math shows all math-related blocks, like the **+** block, which lets you add numbers, and the **/** block, which lets you divide them.

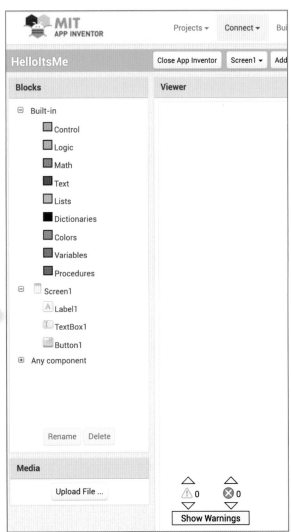

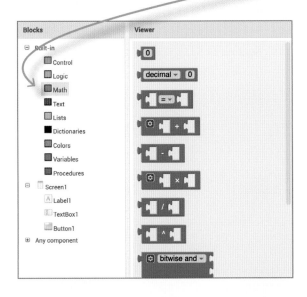

Component Blocks

Component blocks match up with the components that you've added. As soon as you add a component in the Designer, it will automatically appear here too, with its own set of blocks that control the component's behaviors, properties, and actions. Click on a component to make its available blocks appear. For example, clicking on **Button1** shows all the blocks you can use that control the behavior of that button, or what should happen when a user clicks or touches the button.

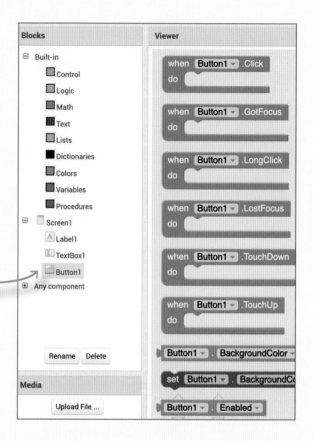

If you click on **Label1**, you'll see that it doesn't have any gold event blocks, because you can't click or touch a label to make it do something the way you can with a button. But you'll see that labels do have green blocks, which set their properties.

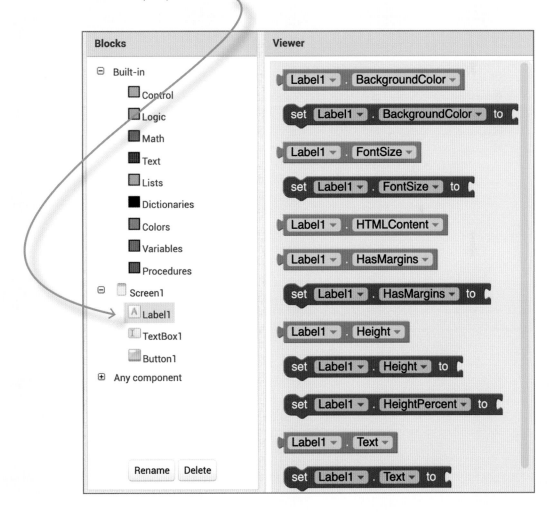

For both Built-in blocks and Component
blocks, click and drag them into the Viewer
panel to make them part of your app.

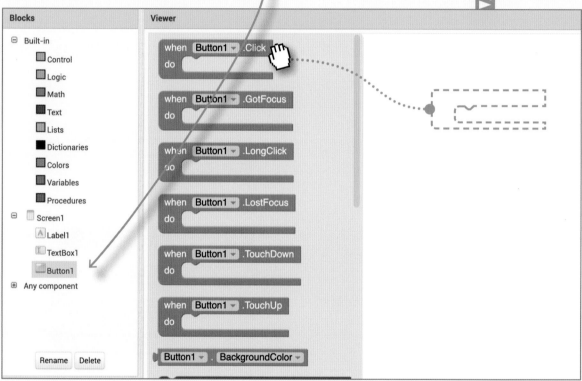

By adding blocks and snapping them together, you'll create a set of instructions. And that's how you'll build apps.

Now that you know the basics, are you ready to get started?

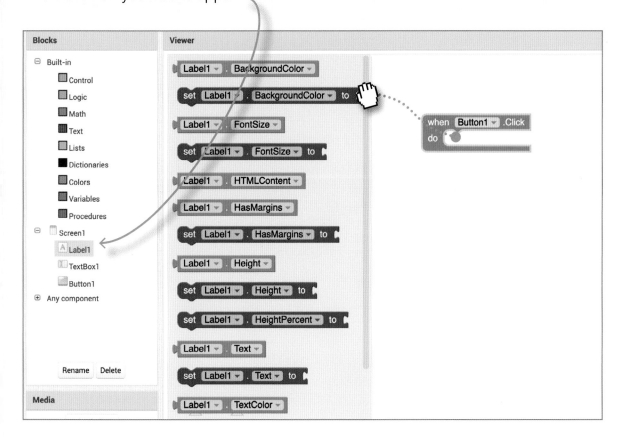

TWO SISTERS

Bethany: Hi there, coders! We are sisters. I'm Bethany, and I'm fifteen.

Ice: I'm Ice, and I'm twelve. When I was small, I loved exploring the machines and devices at home. Sometimes I break stuff when I'm exploring.

Bethany: Oh, so you were the one who broke the radio by putting a coin into it.

Ice: That's not the point. I fixed some of the other machines before you or our parents even noticed. Anyway, then we got this really cool machine called the computer! I was overjoyed and immediately I loved it. Whenever I found some new apps or websites, I explored ways to use them without the user manual. When I was about nine, I was introduced to coding. We made a robot car move around by tapping a button! I thought it was seriously cool—and then I joined the CoolThink@JC competition and was introduced to App Inventor 2 (AI2) by my IT teacher in April 2019.

Bethany: At that time, Ice got to learn how to code on AI2, and when she got home, she proudly showed us her apps. I got interested in AI2

Bethany and Ice

as well. I asked her to teach me the basics that summer. In a few days, I had become a level 1 beginner AI2 coder.

Ice: That summer, we created an app together with five games to play on our vacation. It was awesome! Although our games were very basic and simple, we felt extremely triumphant because we created them ourselves and it was fun to work together.

Bethany: After that, whenever we were free, we also experimented with some other functions of AI2 and carried on with creating new games.

Ice: Life was all right, but then the COVID-19 pandemic spread across the globe. We couldn't go to school or go out, so we gradually became bored and unmotivated. "What can we do during this pandemic?" we pondered. One afternoon, I scrolled through the App Inventor website—they had announced a monthly Coronavirus App Challenge! We were like, whoa!

Bethany: That same night, we brainstormed some concepts for the challenge, and suddenly a great idea popped into our minds. Why not create an app with games to defeat virtual viruses? That would be fun to make and also raise users' awareness of hygiene! We squealed in excitement and gave each other high fives.

Ice: The next few weeks we started to make our app. It has a checklist of habits to keep clean and healthy, which gets you points; a small game to get more points; and a "Virus Battle" page to kill virtual viruses with some spray you can buy with your points. It also has pages for seeing all the viruses you defeated and for facts about the pandemic. Plus there's a detailed user manual.

Bethany: We planned to add a lot of colorful illustrations and interesting cartoons in the app, but we were worried that we couldn't finish all of them in time! We worked out a huge plan where we would draw the illustrations with our phones and code a little after we had finished our online homework.

Ice: After drawing all of the pictures, we had already coded nearly a quarter of the app. We worked together in front of our computer, dragging components and blocks across the screen while calculating the required values and testing out the app using the emulator. Finally, after two weeks, our app was completed!

Bethany: Our success didn't come to us overnight. In fact, we faced a lot of problems while making the app. For instance, we were frustrated when we spent almost three hours trying to figure out some calculations for the game! At that point, we stopped working on that part for a while and had a little rest. Then we went back and eventually thought of a solution!

Ice: We submitted our app to the MIT App Inventor website and we became the MIT App Inventor Coronavirus App Challenge Young Inventors of the Month! We were absolutely ecstatic!

Bethany: Later we did a brief reflection of our app-making process. We concluded that we learned more AI2 techniques and functions, and to never to give up because there is always a way to solve our problems.

Ice: More important, we understood how to work as a team. We got past our differences and respected the other person's opinions because we were eager to finish our app together. Our sisterly bond has been enhanced greatly! Our minds are practically in sync these days!

Bethany: To sum up, we are incredibly grateful to have this chance to express our ideas through coding.

Ice: We would like to thank our parents, who gave us encouragement and support, as well as my IT teacher for introducing me to App Inventor, coding, and STEM.

Bethany: And we sincerely thank MIT for giving us an App of the Month award. It means a lot to us and it has motivated us to continue coding on App Inventor 2!

Ice: If any frustrated coder is flipping through these pages and trying to solve a bug in your app, here is some advice: relax! Don't let it make you angry or tired. Instead, take a rest, give your brain time to think about the problem, go through your codes calmly, and maybe have a snack or two . . .

Bethany: Then ta-da! Inspiration strikes! You snap your fingers and say, "I know what's wrong now!" and find a solution to your bug. Debugging complete!

Ice: Happy coding!

CHAPTER 2

Hello, It's Me!

Do you have relatives and friends who live far away? They might enjoy seeing your face and hearing your voice when you can't be with them. In this app, HelloItsMe, your picture will appear, and when the user clicks on it, they'll hear you greeting them!

Prepare Your Assets

Assets are extra files, like images and sounds, that are part of an app. For this app, you will be adding two assets: an image (of yourself) and a sound (your voice). Start by finding a good digital picture of your face and saving it somewhere on your computer where you can find it later, like your desktop. If you don't have one already, you can take a picture with your computer. If you're on a Mac computer, use the Photo Booth app. Take a picture, then under the File menu, choose Export and save it to your desktop. When you save the file, name it so you can easily find it again. If you're on a Windows computer, use the Camera app. When you take a picture, it's automatically saved in the Camera Roll folder inside the Pictures folder on your computer. Don't forget to smile for the camera!

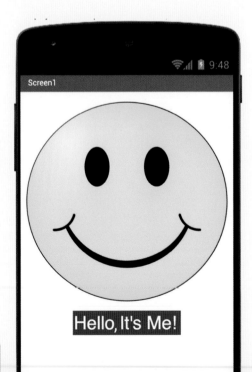

Hello, It's Me!

The second thing you need is a recording of your voice. Think of a good greeting or message for your friends and family. It can be something simple like "Hi, it's me! Wanted to say hello and wish you a happy day!" or you can record something a bit longer: "Hello, my name is Codi. I am a big fan of biking, skating, and programming apps. This is my first app. I hope you like it!" Feel free to get creative! If you use a Mac, the QuickTime application is an easy way to record your voice. Just go to the File menu and choose Audio Recording. If you use a Windows computer, you can record your voice using the Sound Recorder app. In both cases, make sure to save your recording on your computer where you can find it later.

If you don't have MIT App Inventor already open from chapter 1, use a browser on your computer to open it up by going to either http://ai2.appinventor.mit.edu (with your Gmail account) or http://code.appinventor .mit.edu (with your return code).

Open Your Project

1) If your HelloItsMe project isn't already open, go to the Projects menu and select My projects from the drop-down options.

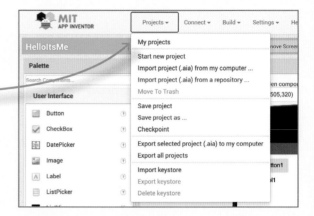

2) Click on HelloItsMe in the project list to open it.

Your project should open in the Designer window, but if it doesn't, just click the (Designer) button in the upper-right corner.

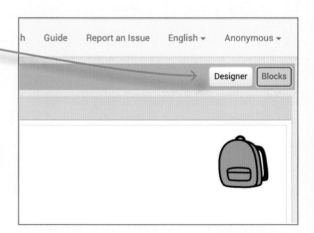

3) If you have any components left over from following along in chapter 1, you'll need to delete them by clicking on each component in the Components panel and then clicking the (Delete) button. You'll be asked to confirm that you really want to delete them.

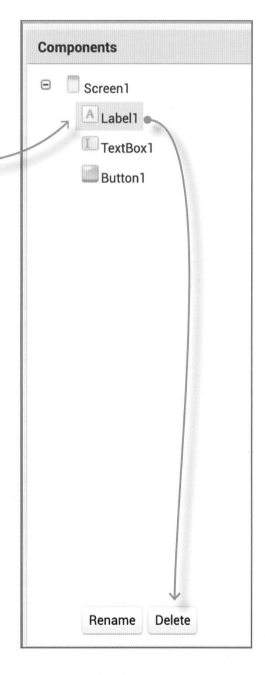

Add the Components

4) Add a **Button** and a **Label**
   component to your app by dragging
   them from the User Interface drawer in
   the Palette to the Viewer.

5) Now click on the Media tab in the Palette and drag a **Player** component onto the Viewer.

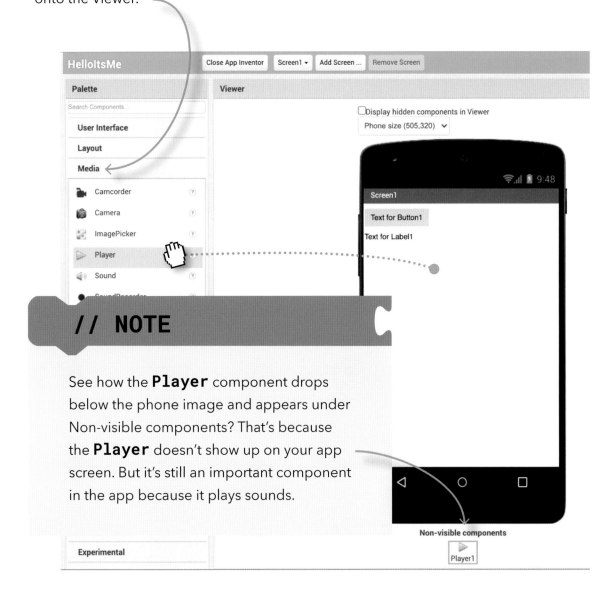

Add Image and Voice Files to Your App

Now it's time to upload your picture and voice recording to App Inventor.

6) Find the Media panel, which is below the Components panel. Click on the (Upload File ...) button. Then click the (Choose File) button, locate the image of yourself on your computer, and click (OK) to upload it. Then repeat those steps for your voice recording. Both of your files will then appear in the Media panel as assets.

Components

Screen1
- Button1
- Label1
- Player1

Rename   Delete

Media

Upload File ...

Screen1

9:48

Upload File ...

Choose File   No file chosen

Cancel   OK

Change the Component Properties

Let's change some of the properties of the components to make the app look better.

7) Click on **Button1** in the Components panel and change the **Button1** properties in the Properties panel like this:

<u>Height</u>: 300 pixels
<u>Width</u>: Fill parent

// NOTE

Remember, properties are different characteristics of a component that you can change to alter how the component looks. Properties include things like width, height, color, and visibility.

// NOTE

You can tell which component is the **parent** by looking at the Components panel. See how **Button1**, **Label1**, and **Player1** are all indented under **Screen1**? That means that **Screen1** is the parent, and **Button1**, **Label1**, and **Player1** are **Screen1**'s **children**. You can think of a container as a parent and any components inside the container as children.

Fill parent means to make the property, in this case the width of **Button1**, the same as its parent. **Button1**'s parent is **Screen1**, because **Button1** is contained within **Screen1**. So you are setting the width of **Button1** to the same width as **Screen1**.

8) The next step is to find Image in the Properties panel and click None…. Choose the image file that you uploaded earlier, then click OK to use your image as the background for **Button1**. Once you choose the image file, the image will appear on the button in the Viewer.

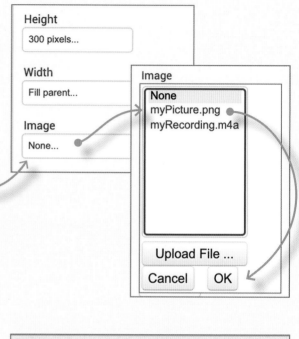

9) Choose **Player1** from the Components list and set its Source property to the voice recording file that you uploaded earlier. Then click OK to use your sound file as the source when it plays. This will attach the sound file to the Player, so when the Player is started in the app, it knows which sound to play.

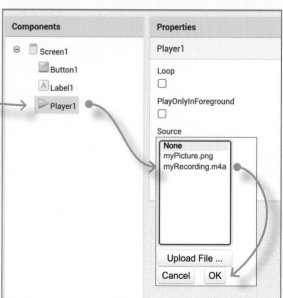

10) Click on **Label1** in the Components list and change the Label properties:
BackgroundColor: *Choose a color*
FontSize: 30
Text: **Press Me**
TextColor: *Choose a color*

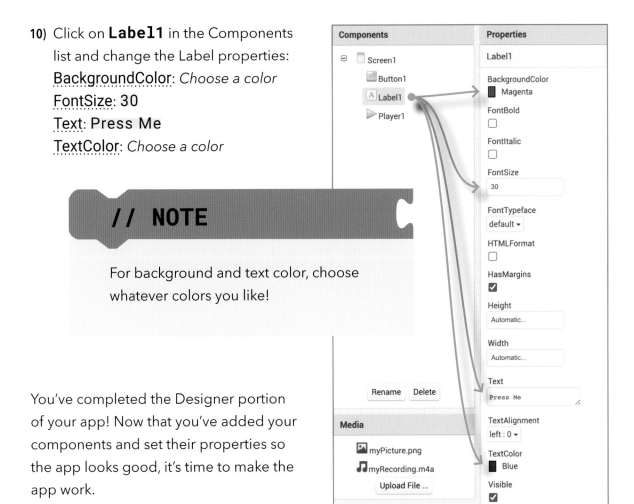

// NOTE

For background and text color, choose whatever colors you like!

You've completed the Designer portion of your app! Now that you've added your components and set their properties so the app looks good, it's time to make the app work.

Code the Blocks

Your app has all its components, but it doesn't do anything yet. Now is your chance to code the app so it works when the user runs it.

11) Click on the (Blocks) button in the upper-right corner of the screen to switch to the Blocks Editor.

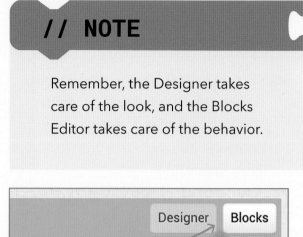

// NOTE

Remember, the Designer takes care of the look, and the Blocks Editor takes care of the behavior.

In the app, you want your voice recording to play when the user presses on your picture, which is displayed on **Button1**. Clicking or pressing a button is called an **event**. When an event happens, it should trigger an action. In this case, the event of clicking on your picture should make your voice recording play. In the **Button1** blocks, the gold ones with an empty area in the middle are called **event handlers**. Event handlers do just that—they handle events. When an event happens in an app, the code blocks inside the event handler tell the app what actions should happen.

For example, in the following code blocks, when the user clicks on **Button1**, the text for **Label1** is set to Hello World! You can add as many blocks as you want inside the **when Button1.Click** event block. All the blocks inside will run whenever the user clicks on the button.

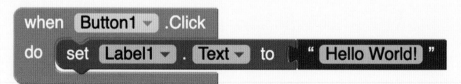

12) If you click on **Button1** in the Blocks palette, you can see the blocks available for **Button1**. Drag out the block called **when Button1.Click**.

When a user clicks on **Button1** in the app, this block will be activated and whatever blocks are inside this event block will run.

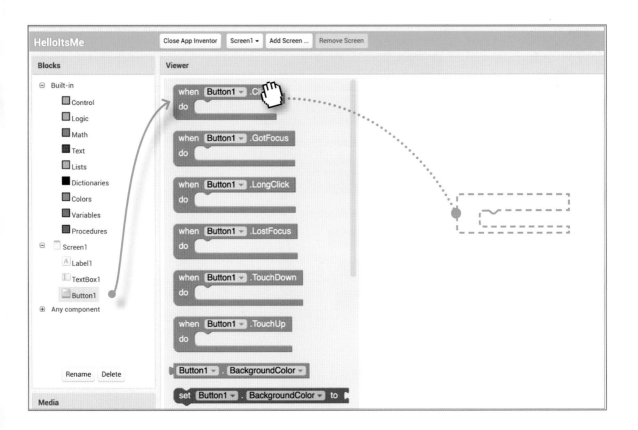

The purple blocks are action blocks. When the user clicks on **Button1** (your picture), you want the Player to start your voice recording.

13) Click on **Player1** in the Blocks palette on the left, drag out the **call Player1.Start** block, and snap it into the **when Button1.Click** block.

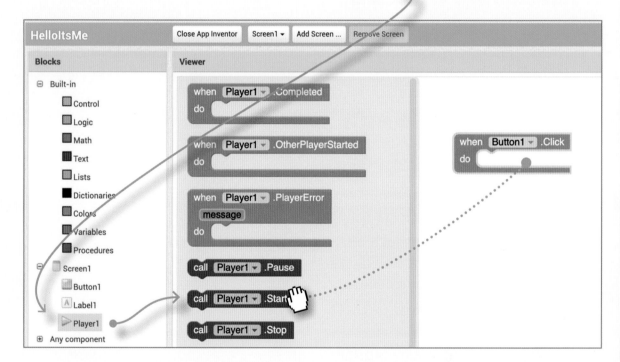

Test Your App

Now it's time to test your app!

14) On your mobile device, either a phone or a tablet, find the MIT AI2 Companion app that you already installed and open it up.

It should look like this:

15) Click the blue button that says scan QR code.

16) On your computer, go to MIT App Inventor, open the Connect menu, and click on AI Companion from the drop-down options. A pop-up window will appear on your computer with a QR code. Scan the QR code that appears with your mobile device that is running the AI2 Companion.

If you don't have a mobile device with good Wi-Fi, you can also test by choosing the Emulator or USB options from the Connect menu.

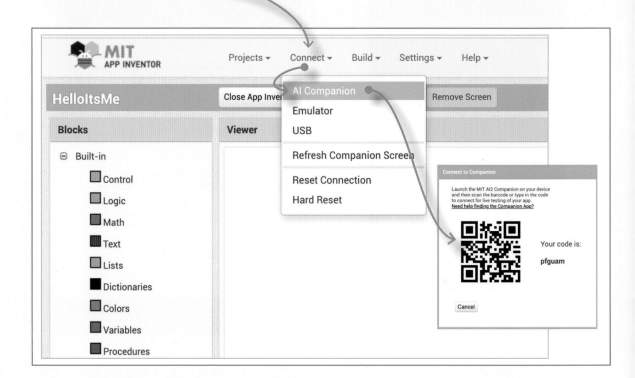

See your app on your mobile device screen? Press the picture of yourself in the app and listen to your voice recording. Make sure the sound is turned on!

Congratulations! You've made your first mobile app!

Extend Your App

Now that you've built your first app, think about adding some new features! You could:

- Change the background color of **Screen1**.

- Add a label with your name.

- Add a second button for another person's picture and recording.

What other ideas do you have? Feel free to try them out.

APA PURA

In Moldova, a small landlocked country in Eastern Europe, lack of clean drinking water is a major problem. Many Moldovans get their water from wells, but about 80 percent of the country's wells don't meet standards for safe drinking water. In fact, many of the wells have high amounts of heavy metals and *E. coli*, a type of bacteria that can make people sick.

The village of Ştefăneşti, Moldova, is in one of the areas most affected by contaminated water. In Ştefăneşti, people go to a local well and fill buckets with water to carry home and use for drinking and cooking. The town has one of the highest rates of children with hepatitis A, a contagious disease that comes from drinking unclean water. Hepatitis A affects the liver and can cause flu-like symptoms and extreme tiredness.

Five teenage girls from Ştefăneşti

THEY LEARNED THAT IN THE PREVIOUS YEAR, SIXTY-SEVEN KIDS IN THEIR SCHOOL HAD CONTRACTED HEPATITIS A.

set out to help. First they did some research and talked to their school's principal and their mayor. They learned that in the previous year, sixty-seven kids in their school had contracted hepatitis A.

The five girls—Mihaela Birca, Anna Grosu, Corina Hariton, Tatiana Moraru, and Maria Toma—decided to build an app to help prevent the spread of hepatitis A by providing information about water quality. They called the app Apa Pura.

Apa Pura uses a map with markers for different wells, and users can click on a marker to learn about that well's water quality. Each well's water is rated on a scale of 1 to 5 for its appearance, smell, and taste. The app also has pictures of the wells so users can identify them more easily. Whenever a user adds a new well to the app, they report on the quality, add a photo, and can type in notes for other users. The girls placed QR codes near local wells to make it easy for

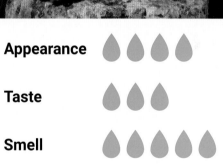

people to download the app.

Another key feature of the app is the information it provides about how to treat water to make it safer to drink. Articles and videos are included to help people understand how to stay safe and healthy when it comes to their drinking water.

The girls' hard work paid off. They entered their app in the Technovation Challenge, a global contest where teams of girls design and build apps that can help their communities. In 2014, they were chosen as finalists and traveled to San Francisco, where they won first place from among nearly nine hundred teams. They were awarded $10,000 to take their app to its next phase of development.

The girls continued to work on their app, eventually renaming it Aquamea. As local stars in their village, they were interviewed on TV and in the newspaper.

Aquamea made their community and their country safer. The experience of designing and building the app improved not only the girls' coding abilities but also their confidence in talking to others and presenting their work. It made them believe in the power of their own ideas.

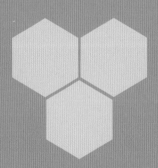

Translation App

This app is inspired by a girl named Amanda who lives in California. Her mother is an immigrant, and sometimes Amanda acts as a translator because her mother isn't confident speaking English. Amanda is proud of her mom and wants her to be able to communicate more easily, and apps like this one can help. This simple translation app is a powerful tool for anyone struggling to communicate with someone who speaks a different language. The user types in a word or phrase and presses the button, and the translated text is displayed.

Let's get started making this cool app!

1) Open MIT App Inventor by using a browser on your computer and going to either http://ai2.appinventor.mit.edu (with Gmail account) or http://code .appinventor.mit.edu (with return code).

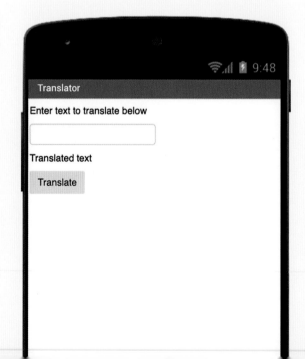

Start a New Project

2) Go to the Projects menu and select Start new project.

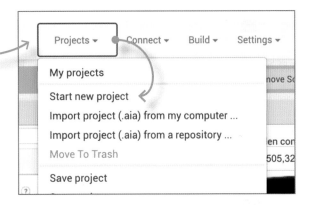

3) Name your new project **TranslationApp**.

Add the Components

Next you'll add the different components that will make up the user interface for your app. The **user interface** is the part of your app that the user interacts with. Whenever you're building an app, it's important to think about *how* you want the app to work, because this will help you decide what components you'll need.

In this app, the user needs a place to type the text and a way to tell the app to translate that text. So you'll need a text box for the user to type in a word or sentence and a button to press as a way to say, "OK, now translate that." It will also be helpful to have labels so the user knows how to work the app.

4)   In the User Interface drawer, drag a **Label**, a **TextBox**, another **Label**, and a **Button** onto the Viewer.

Rename the Components

5) Click on **Label1** and then click the (Rename) button to change its name to InstructionLabel, since it will display instructions for the user.

6) Rename the other components like this:

TextBox1 → InputTextBox
Label2 → TranslationLabel
Button1 → TranslateButton

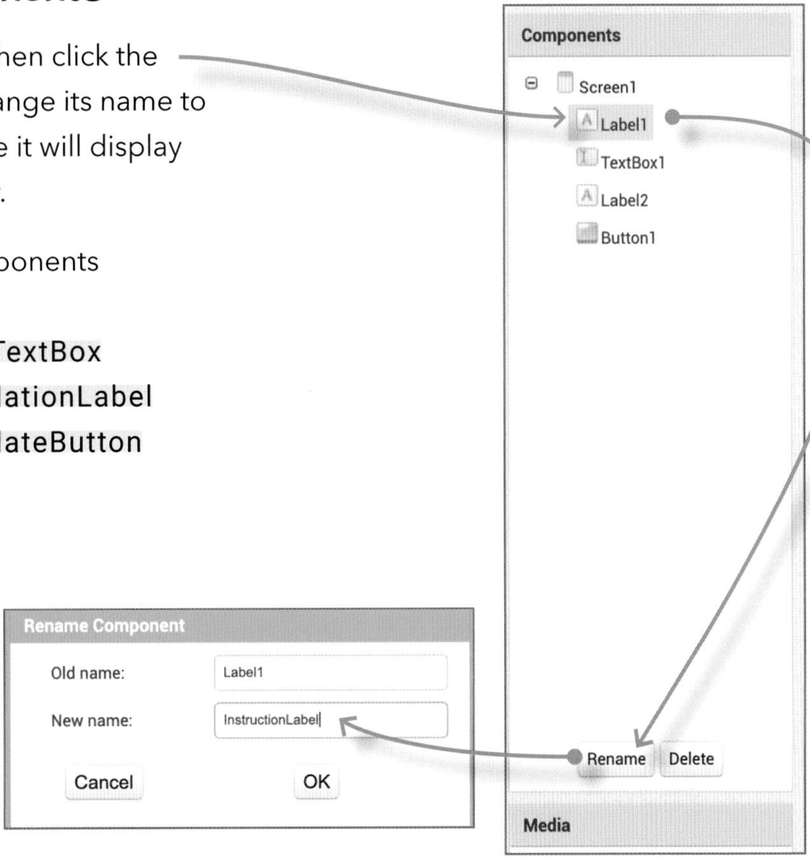

Components

- Screen1
  - Label1
  - TextBox1
  - Label2
  - Button1

Rename Component

Old name:	Label1
New name:	InstructionLabel

Cancel   OK

Rename   Delete

Media

Chapter 3—Translation App

Change the Component Properties

7) Change the Text property of the following components as shown below. This will be the text that each component displays.

InstructionLabel: Enter text to translate below

TranslationLabel: Translated text

TranslateButton: Translate

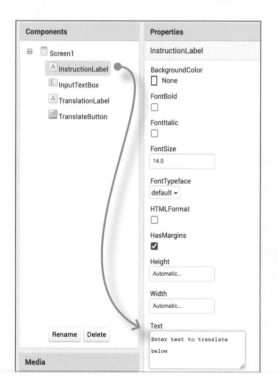

8) You can also change the Title property for **Screen1** to Translator, so that title appears at the top of the app.

This is what your Viewer should look like now:

Add the Translation Component

There's still something missing from the design of your app . . . and that's a way to actually do the translation! Luckily, App Inventor has a component called **YandexTranslate**, which uses the Yandex translation service to translate text from one language to another.

9) Click on the Media tab on the left to open that drawer, drag out a **YandexTranslate** component, and drop it into the Viewer. This is a non-visible component, so it appears below the phone screen in the Viewer.

Congrats! You've finished the Designer part of your app and have all the components you'll need. The next step is to tell the app what *actions* it needs to do, so it's time to code your app in the Blocks Editor.

Code the Translation

10) Click on the (Blocks) button in the top right of your screen to go to the Blocks Editor.

Designer   Blocks

Properties

Just as with the HelloItsMe app, you want your translator app to do something when the user presses a button, in this case the **TranslateButton**. So you want to code the event handler for when the user clicks **TranslateButton**.

// NOTE

Remember, event handler blocks tell your app what actions should happen when an event happens. The event in this case is the user clicking the **TranslateButton**.

11) Click on **TranslateButton** in the Blocks palette on the left to show its available blocks, then click the **when TranslateButton.Click** event block and drag it into the Viewer area.

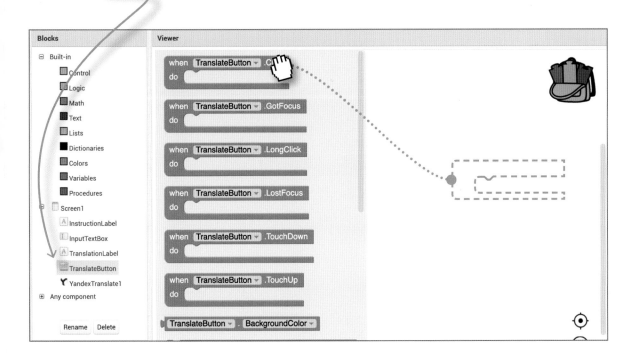

What action should happen when the user clicks on the button? You want the words in the text box to get translated, and for the translated text to be displayed. Take a look at the available blocks for the **YandexTranslate** component.

12) Drag out a **`call YandexTranslate1.`** **`RequestTranslation`** block and snap it into the **when TranslateButton.Click** block.

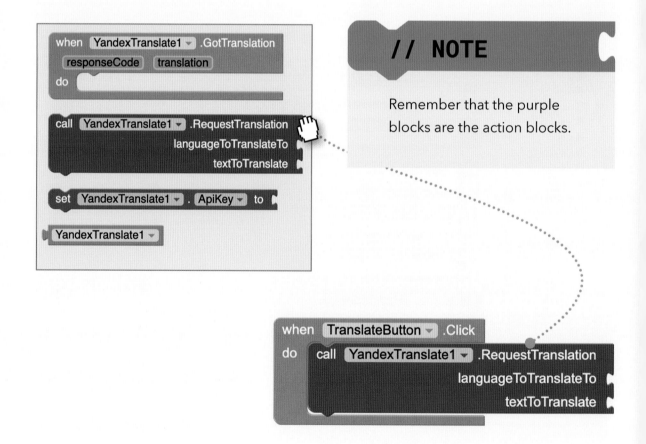

// NOTE

Remember that the purple blocks are the action blocks.

See the two empty puzzle slots in the **`call YandexTranslate1.`** **`RequestTranslation`** block? You need to fill in those empty puzzle pieces because the Yandex translator needs a bit more information to do the translation. Those empty puzzle pieces represent **input parameters**. Input parameters are information you pass to a block. That information gives the block what it needs to do its job. For this **`RequestTranslation`** block, it needs to know:

- **`languageToTranslateTo`** and

- **`textToTranslate`**

For **`languageToTranslateTo`**, you need to tell the translator the language being input, as well as the language you want output. Let's translate from English to Spanish.

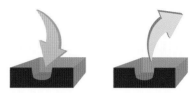

// NOTE

Input and **output** are important concepts in computer science. Input is information that goes *in*, and output is info that comes *out*. You can input information to a computer by typing, talking, or pressing buttons. In code blocks, you can input information by using input parameters. Computer programs output things like words, sounds, and images. Code blocks can also output information, like translated text.

The **YandexTranslate** component uses codes to specify the languages.

The code for English is *en* and the code for Spanish is *es*. So `en-es` will be the `languageToTranslateTo`, since we're translating from English to Spanish.

If you want to translate between other languages, just change the codes. For example, if you wanted to translate from Japanese to Chinese, you would use *ja-zh*.

Language	Code	Language	Code	Language	Code	Language	Code
Azerbaijani	az	Malayalam	ml	Danish	da	Tajik	tg
Albanian	sq	Maltese	mt	Hebrew	he	Thai	th
Amharic	am	Macedonian	mk	Yiddish	yi	Tagalog	tl
English	en	Maori	mi	Indonesian	id	Tamil	ta
Arabic	ar	Marathi	mr	Irish	ga	Tartar	tt
Armenian	hy	Mari	mhr	Italian	it	Telugu	te
Afrikaans	af	Mongolian	mn	Icelandic	is	Turkish	tr
Basque	eu	German	de	Spanish	es	Udmurt	udm
Bashkir	ba	Nepalese	ne	Kazakh	kk	Uzbek	uz
Belarusian	be	Norwegian	no	Kannada	kn	Ukrainian	uk
Bengal	bn	Punjabi	pa	Catalan	ca	Urdu	ur
Burmese	my	Papiamento	pap	Kirghiz	ky	Finnish	fi
Bulgarian	bg	Persian	fa	Chinese	zh	French	fr
Bosnian	bs	Polish	pl	Korean	ko	Hindi	hi
Welsh	cy	Portuguese	pt	Xhosa	xh	Croatian	hr
Hungarian	hu	Romanian	ro	Khmer	km	Czech	cs
Vietnamese	vi	Russian	ru	Laotian	lo	Swedish	sv
Haitian (Creole)	ht	Cebuano	ceb	Latin	la	Scottish	gd
Galician	gl	Serbian	sr	Latvian	lv	Estonian	et
Dutch	nl	Sinhalese	si	Lithuanian	lt	Esperanto	eo
Hill Mari	mrj	Slovak	sk	Luxembourg	lb	Javanese	jv
Greek	el	Slovenian	sl	Malagasy	mg	Japanese	ja
Georgian	ka	Swahili	sw	Malay	ms		
Gujarati	gu	Sundanese	su				

(from https://tech.yandex.com/translate/doc/dg/concepts/api-overview-docpage/)

13) From the Text drawer in the Blocks palette, grab a blank text block and snap it into the **`languageToTranslateTo`** slot. Type **en-es** into the empty text block.

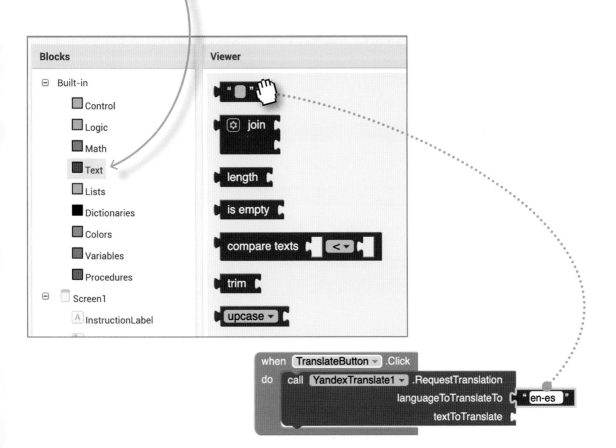

textToTranslate is what you want translated. In this case, it's the text the user typed in the text box, so you'll need to use **InputTextBox.Text**. This pulls the text that the user has typed and tells the program that's what it should translate.

14) Click on **InputTextBox** in the Blocks palette and find the lighter green **InputTextBox.Text** block. Drag it out and snap it into the **textToTranslate** slot.

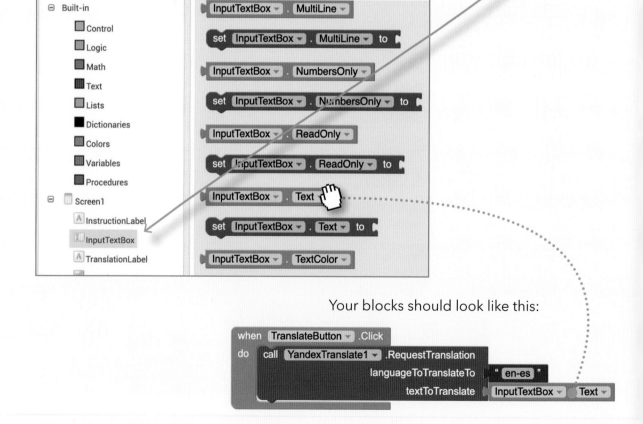

Your blocks should look like this:

The **YandexTranslate** component asks for the translation, and then it has to wait for a response. When the Yandex translation service responds, a **GotTranslation** event is triggered. **GotTranslation** is a different type of event; it's triggered by Yandex saying, "Hey, I'm done—here's the output you asked for." Then the app can take that output (the translation) to display it in a label for the user to read.

15) Drag out a **when YandexTranslate1. GotTranslation** block.

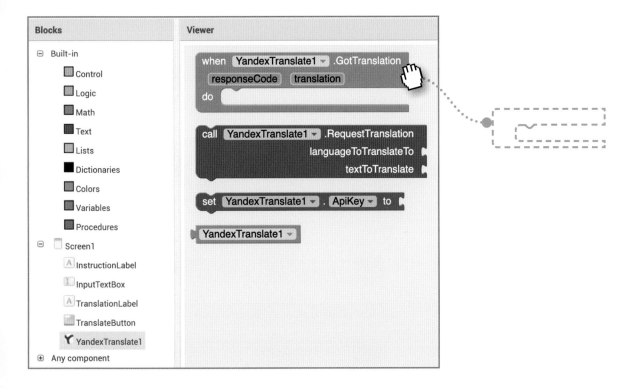

Once the app receives the translation, what needs to happen? The user needs to see the translation. Think about where you want the translation displayed.

16) Click on **TranslationLabel**, drag out a dark green **set TranslationLabel.Text** block, and snap it into the **when YandexTranslate1. GotTranslation** block.

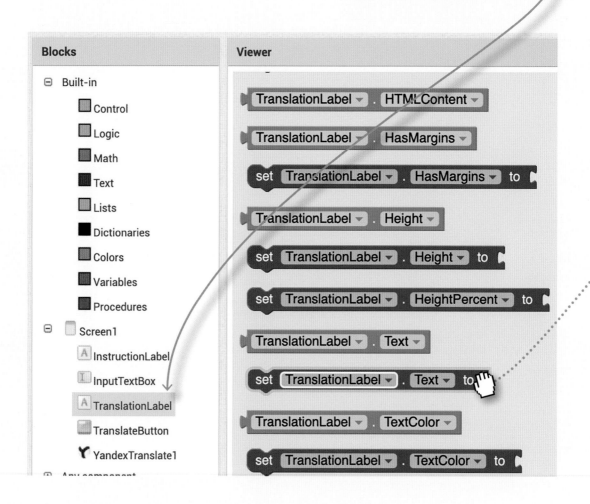

See the two orange buttons in the gold **when YandexTranslate1. GotTranslation** block? They represent information that the translator sent in response to the request. These are output from the translator. In this case, the translator is sending two pieces of information.

The first piece is the **responseCode**, a number that would tell you if there was an error in translating.

The other output information from the translator is the translated text. That's what you want to display.

17) Hover over the orange **translation** button, grab the **get translation** block that appears, and snap it into the open slot in **set TranslationLabel.Text**.

The finished blocks will look like this:

With very few blocks, you've done quite a bit! When the user clicks on the (Translate) button, the app asks the Yandex translator to translate the words in the text box from English to Spanish. The translator receives the app's request, does its thing, and responds in **GotTranslation** with the translated text. The app then displays the translation in the **TranslationLabel** so the user can read it.

Test Your App

Now it's time to see how your app works!

18) On your mobile device, either a phone or a tablet, find the MIT AI2 Companion app that you've already downloaded and open it up.

19) On your computer, go to MIT App Inventor, open the Connect menu, and click on AI Companion from the drop-down menu. A pop-up window with a QR code will appear on your computer. Scan the QR code with your mobile device.

20) Type a word or phrase into the text box and press the (Translate) button. Does it translate to Spanish correctly?

21) Try more words and sentences to make sure the app works correctly. It's always good to test your app out thoroughly so you know it works.

Congratulations! You've made your own personal translation app. Way to go!

Extend Your App

How about expanding your app? You could try the following:

- Change which language you translate to (or from). Use the Yandex language codes to change the languages your app uses.

- Add more buttons for different languages. You could keep your original (Translate) button as the Spanish button and add another button to translate to French!

- Add a **TextToSpeech** component so your device speaks the translation out loud in addition to displaying it. Note that if you want it to speak in a different language, you must change the Country and Language properties to match the country and language you want.

What other ideas do you have? Try them!

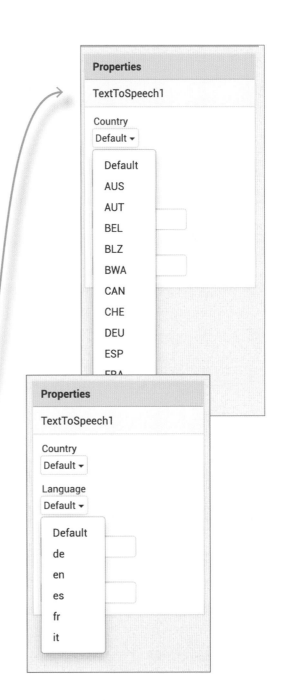

VANESSA'S STORY

Vanessa Tostado was introduced to coding in high school. She'd always done well in math and science, so on her first day of computer science class, she went in feeling confident and comfortable. She quickly realized she was in over her head. Often she would have to stay in during lunch to finish assignments, and she was one of the only girls in her class. She felt out of place and incapable and became convinced she wasn't cut out to learn coding.

Still, she mustered the courage to participate in the Technovation Challenge, which requires girls to identify a problem in their community

HER DESIRE TO MAKE AN IMPACT ON THE COMMUNITY SILENCED THE VOICE TELLING HER SHE DIDN'T BELONG IN THE TECHNOLOGY SPACE.

and make an app to help address it. Her desire to make an impact on the community silenced the voice telling her she didn't belong in the technology space. Along with three other girls from East Palo Alto, California—Ashley Davis, Margarita Tenisi, and Rosie Valencia—Vanessa created an app called Tag It, which encourages users to take pictures of vandalized areas and organize cleanups. The four girls called themselves the EPA Chica Squad.

With the help of mentors Sarah Clatterbuck and Selina Martinez, the EPA Chica Squad spent twelve weeks researching, prototyping, and developing Tag It. In the Technovation Challenge, they placed in the top twenty worldwide and the top five out of thirty-six entries in the San Francisco region. The mentorship and positive reinforcement Vanessa received during that time pushed her to apply for LinkedIn's High School Trainee Program. That summer, Vanessa learned the basics of web development and software engineering. With the help of a new mentor, Varun Varada, Vanessa's confidence grew.

In the fall, she began her freshman year at Wesleyan University. She wasn't able to get a spot for Introduction to

Vanessa at her Wesleyan University graduation

Computer Science her first semester, but she didn't give up. After some help from her adviser, she enrolled during her second semester. Vanessa graduated in 2019. Her major? Computer science.

Vanessa was the first person in her family to finish high school and college. Today she works as a software developer. She hopes to inspire and open doors for the next generation of leaders.

CHAPTER 4

My Piano

Do you play a musical instrument? Piano? Violin? Flute? Even if you don't, this is a fun app to make and play.

The app has eight colorful buttons labeled with musical notes. When the user presses a button, the app plays the note.

There is also a label below the buttons that displays each note as the user plays it. The (Clear Notes) button at the bottom allows the user to erase all the notes in the label.

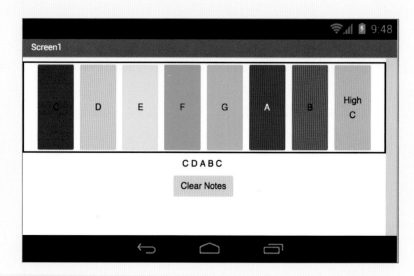

Import the Template

1) Use a browser on your computer to open MIT App Inventor by going to either http://ai2.appinventor.mit.edu (with your Gmail account) or http://code.appinventor.mit.edu (with return code).

2) All your projects live on the App Inventor server, so go to the Projects menu and select My projects to see a list.

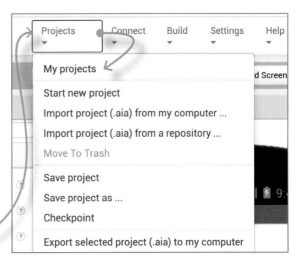

You can click on any project in the list to open it, edit it, and run it.

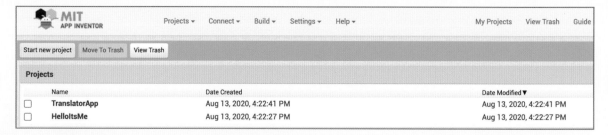

// NOTE

You can also share projects with a friend. If you export the project, save it on your computer, and then email it to your friend, they can import the project and open it in App Inventor on their computer. Then they'll have their own copy of the project to look at and edit themselves.

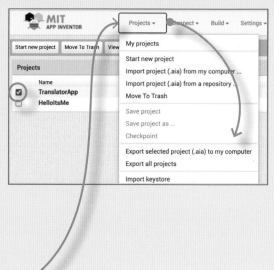

To export a project, you can either open the project first or click the checkbox to the left of the project name in your project list. Then choose Export selected project (.aia) to my computer.

3) To make the MyPiano app, there's a starter project file that you'll need to import to App Inventor. Go to http://appinventor.mit.edu/assets/files/book/MyPiano_template.aia and download the file to your computer. The downloaded file will be named MyPiano_template.aia. The .aia part at the end is called an **extension**. All App Inventor project files have the same .aia extension.

4) In App Inventor, click on the Projects menu and select the Import project (.aia) from my computer … option. When prompted, choose the MyPiano_template.aia file you downloaded to your computer.

The starter project will automatically open, and it will also appear in your list of projects in App Inventor. It should look like an empty project, except that the Media tab will have the musical note sound files you need.

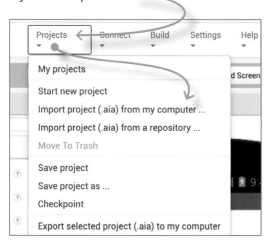

The other thing you'll notice is that the phone in the Viewer panel of the Designer window is horizontal. That means when someone plays the app, they'll hold their phone or tablet horizontally, which is called **landscape mode**. A vertical layout is called **portrait mode**.

You can set your app to landscape or portrait mode in the properties for **Screen1**. Look for the property ScreenOrientation. The default is **Unspecified**, which means the app automatically uses whatever the setting is for your mobile device. By changing the property to **Landscape**, you can make the app appear horizontally, which is perfect for a piano!

PrimaryColor
  Default
PrimaryColorDark
  Default
ScreenOrientation
Unspecified ▾

Unspecified
Portrait
Landscape
Sensor

Add the Components

The plan is to create a piano with eight keys side by side. You may have noticed that when you add components in App Inventor, they are stacked vertically from top to bottom. New components appear below the components you've already added. But for this app, you want the keys to be next to one another, so you'll need to add a **HorizontalArrangement** component from the Layout drawer. A **HorizontalArrangement** creates a box, and if you add components inside that box, they appear side by side.

5) Click on the Layout drawer in the Palette panel on the left, select **HorizontalArrangement**, and drop it into the Viewer.

You want the keys to fill up the entire screen horizontally and about half of the screen vertically. You also want to set the alignment so the keys are centered when they are all added.

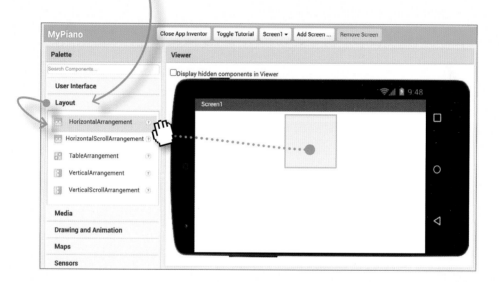

// NOTE

Alignment has to do with how objects are organized on the screen. **Left alignment** means all the objects are arranged along the left edge. **Right alignment** means they're arranged on the right. And **center alignment** means they're all in the middle.

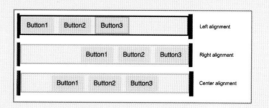

6) Go to the Properties panel for
   HorizontalArrangement1 and
   change its properties as follows:

   - <u>AlignHorizontal</u>: Center: 3

   - <u>Height</u>: 50 percent

   - <u>Width</u>: Fill parent

Properties

HorizontalArrangement1

AlignHorizontal

Center : 3 ▾

AlignVertical

Center : 2 ▾

BackgroundColor

☐ None

Height

50 percent...

Width

Fill parent...

Image

None...

Visible

☑

// NOTE

Remember that Fill parent means to fill to the width
of the parent, which in this case is **Screen1**.

7) Now it's time to add the buttons that will become the piano keys. Drag eight **Buttons** from the User Interface drawer into **HorizontalArrangement1**.

They will appear side by side. As you add more, some will be out of order or hidden off-screen, but don't worry—you'll fix all that in a moment by setting the properties.

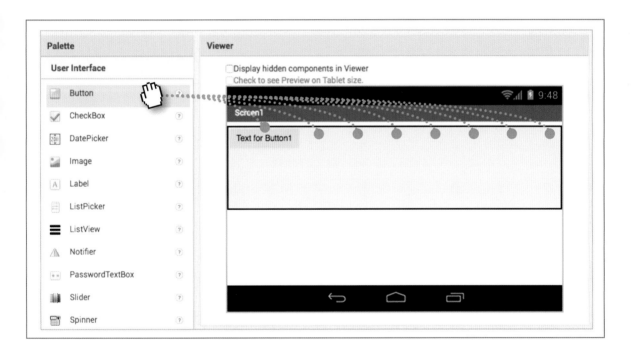

8) Your buttons will be in the same order as the keys on a piano: C, D, E, F, G, A, B, and High C. You'll need to rename them so they match the right notes. Click on **Button1** in the Components panel and change its name to **CNote**.

9) Rename **Button2** DNote.

10) Rename the rest of the buttons in this order: **ENote**, **FNote**, **GNote**, **ANote**, **BNote**, **HighCNote**.

Now that your buttons are renamed, you want to update the properties for them so they all fit on the screen and have proper labels and colorful backgrounds.

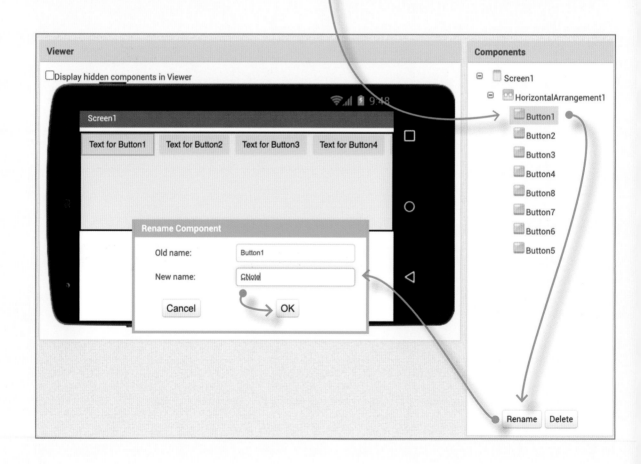

11) Start with the **CNote** and change its properties like this:

- BackgroundColor: Red
- Height: Fill parent
- Width: 10 percent
- Text: C

12) Next, change the properties for **DNote**:

- BackgroundColor: Orange
- Height: Fill parent
- Width: 10 percent
- Text: D

13) Continue changing the remaining keys until your layout looks like the one below.

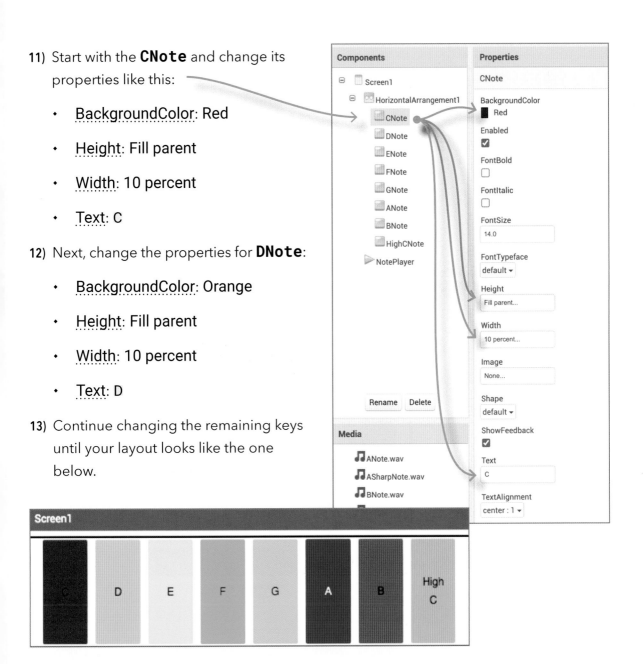

Your app will also show the notes that are played, so you'll need a label. You'll need a button as well, so the user can clear the displayed notes.

14) Drag a **Label** and a **Button** and put them both below **HorizontalArrangement1**.

15) Don't forget that this is a piano app, so you'll need a way to play the notes! From the Media tab, drag a **Player** component onto the Viewer.

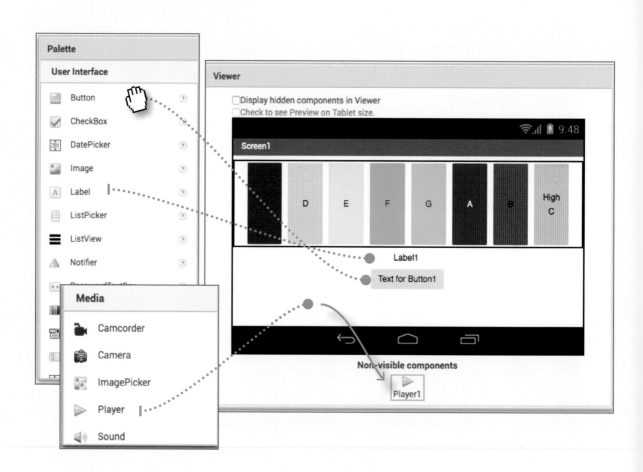

// NOTE

Remember, it's always helpful to give components descriptive names to help you keep track of what they do when you get to the coding part of building your app.

16) Name the **Label** NotesLabel, the **Button** ClearButton, and the **Player** NotePlayer.

17) Erase all the text you see in the Text property for **NotesLabel** so the label is blank.

18) Set the Text property for **ClearButton** to Clear Notes. Your layout should now look like this:

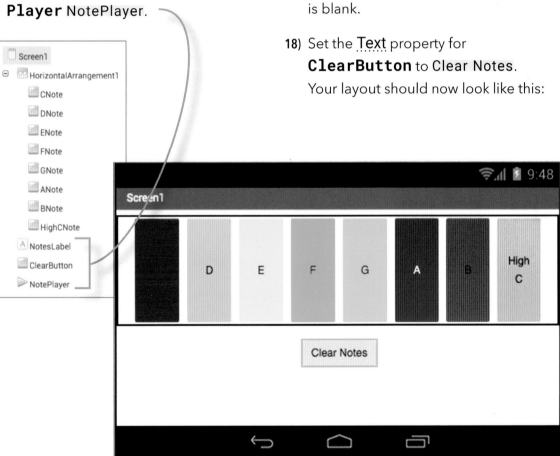

Code the Piano Buttons

That was a lot! But now you're ready to make the app play the notes. Time to move to the Blocks Editor.

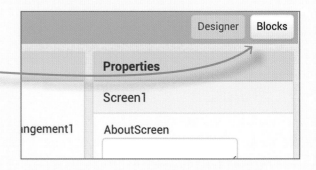

When the user presses a button in the app, the corresponding note should play. Remember in your HelloItsMe app how you uploaded your voice recording and set the **Player**'s Source property to the uploaded recording file? Because that was the only sound the app played, it could be set in the Source property for the **Player** component. In this app, you have several sound files, and the **NotePlayer** has to play a different one depending on which note the user presses. So the Source for the **Player** will have to change whenever the user presses a different note button. You'll have to set the Source for the **Player** in code blocks.

Let's start with the **CNote**.

19) Drag out a `when CNote.Click`
event block.

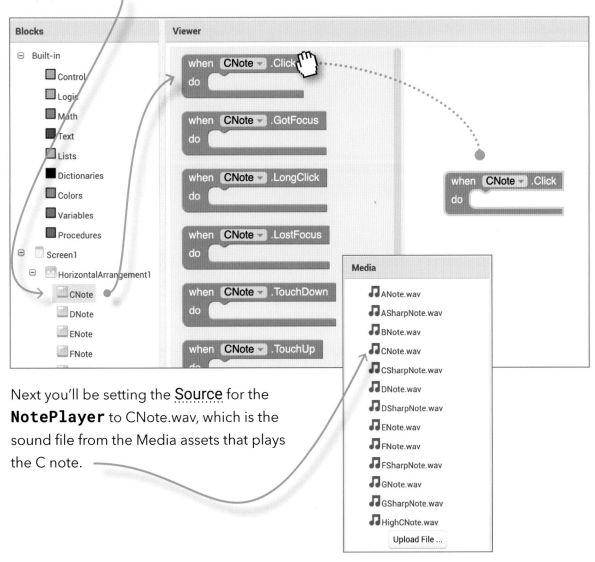

Next you'll be setting the <u>Source</u> for the
NotePlayer to CNote.wav, which is the
sound file from the Media assets that plays
the C note.

20) Drag out a **set NotePlayer. Source** block and snap it into the **when CNote.Click** event block.

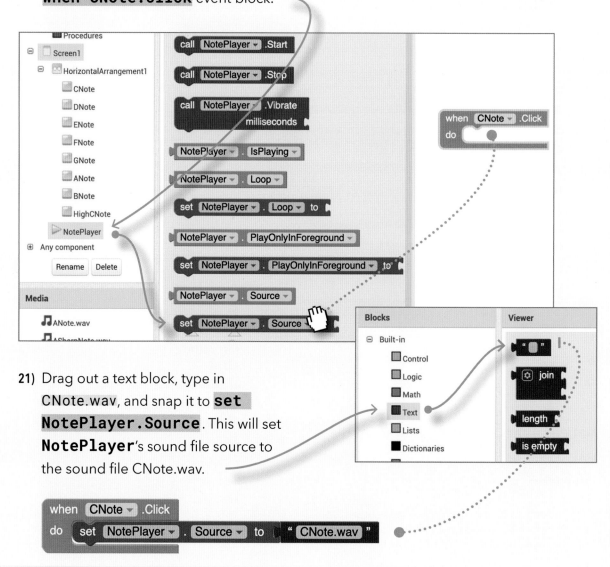

21) Drag out a text block, type in CNote.wav, and snap it to **set NotePlayer.Source**. This will set **NotePlayer**'s sound file source to the sound file CNote.wav.

22) You've set **NotePlayer**'s Source to CNote.wav, so **NotePlayer** knows which sound file to play. Now you need to tell **NotePlayer** to actually play the sound. You'll do that with the purple **call NotePlayer.Start** block. Drag a **call NotePlayer. Start** block out and snap it into **when CNote.Click** below the **set NotePlayer.Source** block.

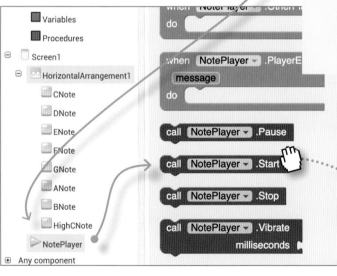

Next, you'll need to display the played note in **NotesLabel**. Changing the Text property will display text in a label. Usually you can do that in the Properties panel in the Designer window, but if you want the text to change while the app is running, you'll need to set the Text property using blocks.

23) For this app, you'll add the block **set NotesLabel.Text** at the end of the event block and snap in a text block with **C** so the letter *C* is displayed in **NotesLabel** on the screen.

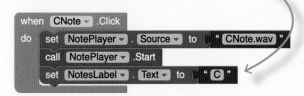

24) Now you're ready to code the other notes! Since most of the code is the same, you can right-click on **when CNote.Click** and choose Duplicate to make a copy of the entire set of blocks.

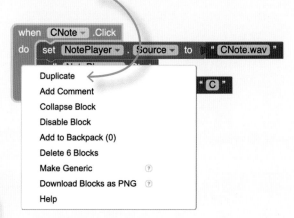

See how there's a red circle with an X in both blocks now? That's because there can be only one **when CNote.Click** event block. You'll fix that now.

when DNote.Click will work almost exactly like **when CNote.Click**, except you'll need to use a different sound file, and you'll want the D note to be displayed instead of the C note.

25) Change **CNote** to **DNote** in the drop-down, and change CNote.wav to DNote.wav and C to D in the text blocks.

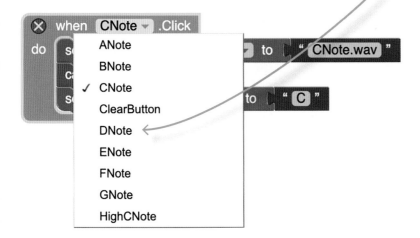

Test Your App

Before you code all eight buttons, it's a smart idea to stop and test. Testing as you go is good programming practice because if something doesn't work the way you want, it's better to fix it before you get too far in the coding.

26) On your mobile device, either a phone or a tablet, find the MIT AI2 Companion app that you already downloaded and open it up.

27) On your computer, open the Connect menu in MIT App Inventor and click on AI Companion from the drop-down menu. A pop-up window with a QR code will appear on your computer. Use your mobile device to scan the code.

28) In the app, try pressing the (C) and (D) buttons. Make sure the volume is turned up! You should hear the different notes and see the **NotesLabel** change. If something doesn't work, go back and check your code blocks to make sure everything is in the right place.

Make a Procedure

You could copy the blocks for each note now, as you did for **DNote**, but there is a better way to code when you have similar code blocks. You can make a **procedure**. A procedure is a set of blocks that you name and wrap up inside a purple action block. You can create your own action block to do a particular task. Then, just as with other action blocks, your procedure can be called in different parts of your program. Remember, whenever you call an action block, the program runs the code inside it.

29) In the Procedures drawer, drag out a **to procedure** block.

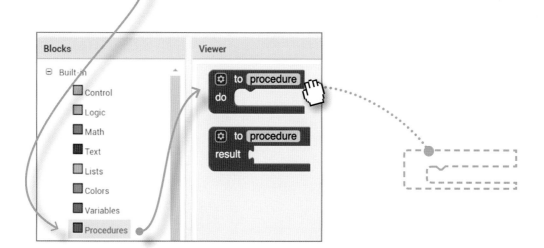

30) Change the name of the procedure to **PlayNote**. Just as with components, it's good practice to name your procedures descriptively so it's clear what each procedure does.

PlayNote needs to know which note will be played, so you will add an input parameter to the procedure. When you call the procedure, you pass it the parameter, giving the procedure the value it needs to run. In this case, you'll pass the note that will be played.

31) Click on the blue gear icon next to **to PlayNote** and then drag **input: x** into the open slot of the block to add the input parameter. Then click on **x**, the default name, and change it to **note**.

32) This procedure should work the same way as **when CNote.Click** and **when DNote.Click**, so drag the code inside the **when CNote.Click** block to the new **PlayNote** procedure block.

Since you want this procedure to play and display the input parameter note, not just C, you'll need to change some things.

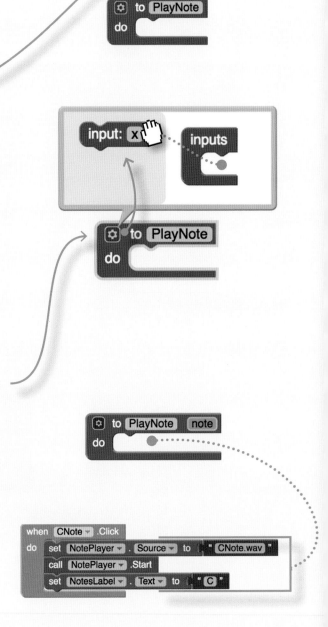

33) Detach the **CNote.wav** text block from **set NotePlayer.Source to** (but don't delete it!) and then drag out a **join** block from the Text drawer. The **join** block does just what it sounds like—it joins two pieces of text together. For example, in joining **C** with **Note.wav**, you get **CNote.wav**, which is exactly what we want when playing the C note.

34) Snap the **join** block to **set NotePlayer.Source to**. Then remove the **C** text block from **set NotesLabel.Text to**. You can leave that in your blocks workspace too.

35) Snap a new text block into the bottom slot of the **join** block, and type in **Note.wav**.

// NOTE

Feel free to pull apart blocks and leave them in your workspace. As long as they're not attached to an event block or a procedure, they won't run, so they won't affect the program. Sometimes it's useful to keep unused blocks handy while coding. When you decide you don't need them, you can right-click and delete them, or drag them to the trash can in the lower right of your screen.

36) Here comes the neat part! Hover over the input parameter, **note**, and drag **get note** into the first empty slot in the **join** block. Then hover again and snap **get note** to **set NotesLabel.Text**.

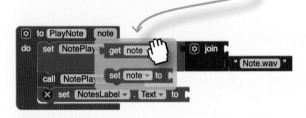

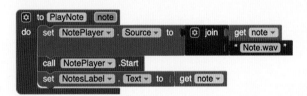

When you call PlayNote with **C** as the input parameter, the **get note** block is replaced with C everywhere it appears in the code blocks. And when you call PlayNote with **D**, **get note** is replaced with D. And so on, for every note! This makes the procedure very adaptable, because it can be used for every note in your piano app.

Call the Procedure

The next thing to do is call the PlayNote procedure from all the **Button.Click** events.

37) Open the Procedures drawer, drag out a **call PlayNote** block, and snap it into the empty **when CNote. Click** block. Your input parameter is **C**, so grab the **C** text block you removed earlier and snap that to **call PlayNote**.

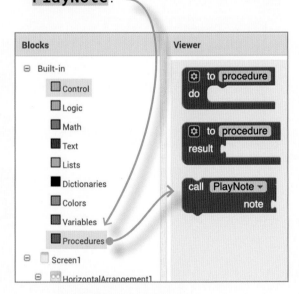

38) Do the same for **when DNote. Click**. Call the PlayNote procedure, and pass it **D** for the input parameter.

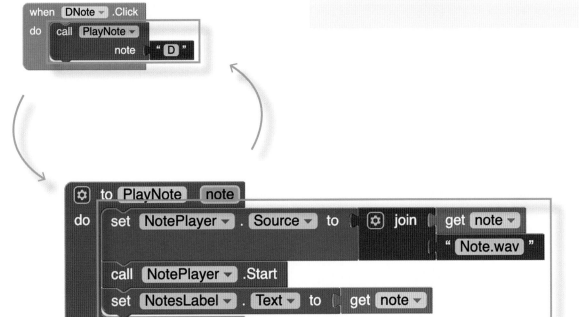

Test Again

39) Keep going until you've finished all the other **Note.Click** event blocks. To be super speedy, you can duplicate the **when CNote.Click** block and then change the button name with the drop-down menu. Don't forget to also change the note input parameter to the correct note. Your code blocks should look like this:

40) Try your app again on your mobile device. Make sure that all the note buttons work, that they play the correct notes, and that the notes are displayed as you play them.

when CNote ▾ .Click
do   call PlayNote ▾
                note " C "

when FNote ▾ .Click
do   call PlayNote ▾
                note " F "

when BNote ▾ .Click
do   call PlayNote ▾
                note " B "

when DNote ▾ .Click
do   call PlayNote ▾
                note " D "

when GNote ▾ .Click
do   call PlayNote ▾
                note " G "

when HighCNote ▾ .Click
do   call PlayNote ▾
                note " HighC "

when ENote ▾ .Click
do   call PlayNote ▾
                note " E "

when ANote ▾ .Click
do   call PlayNote ▾
                note " A "

Update PlayNote

So now you have a very cool piano app. But maybe you want to improve your app by displaying all the notes the user plays instead of just the note that's being played. To do that, you need to update the code block where **NotesLabel.Text** is set to the current note.

Instead of setting **NotesLabel.Text** to just the note being played, you want to add the note to whatever is already displayed in the label. For example, if you play the notes C, D, and E in that order, you would display C D E instead of replacing C with D and then with E.

To do this, you can use the Text **join** block. You'll join three pieces of text together—what's already in **NotesLabel**, a space, and the new note. So, for example, **NotesLabel** might show C D. If the user then plays E, you'd want to join C D and E so it becomes C D E.

// **NOTE**

Here's another benefit to using a procedure to play and display the notes. You only have to update your code in one place, the PlayNote procedure, in order to display all the notes played. If you didn't have the procedure, you'd have to go back to update each **Button.Click** event separately.

41) Find the PlayNote procedure and drag the **get note** block from **set NotesLabel.Text**. Then drag a **join** block from the Text drawer and snap it into place.

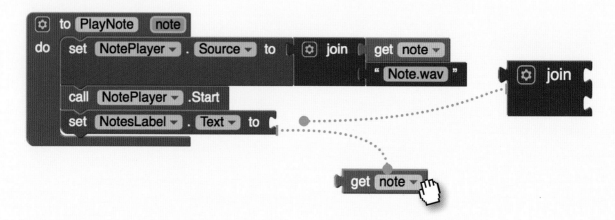

42) Use the blue gear icon on the **join** block to add a third empty slot by dragging over another **string** block.

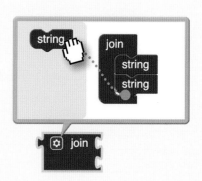

// NOTE

String is another name for text.

43) You want to add to what is already displayed, so drag in the light green **`NotesLabel.Text`** block, which contains the contents of the label. Snap that into the first slot of the **`join`** block.

44) In the middle slot, snap in a blank text block and add a space to it by hitting the spacebar. This will make sure there's a space between the last note and the new note.

45) Snap the **`get note`** block into the third slot.

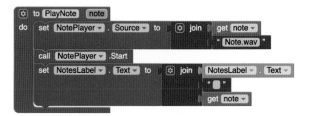

Code the Clear Button

Now that the label displays all of the notes that the user plays, the label can get very long very quickly! It will be helpful to be able to clear it.

46) Drag out a **`when ClearButton. Click`** event block. All you need to do is to make the **`NotesLabel`** blank again. Can you figure out how to do that?

Test Your App

Try it out! Play several notes and check to make sure they're all displayed with spaces in between. Then try pressing Clear Notes and playing more notes.

POTHOLES OF MALDEN

Ryan O'Connell and Daniel Ribeiro are teenagers who live in Malden, Massachusetts, a town just outside of Boston. When their teacher asked them to think about a problem in their school or community and try to fix it with a mobile app, they started brainstorming. Could they make an app to help them remember their class schedules, which changed daily? What about an app to encourage residents to recycle more? But then they had a new idea—potholes!

It was springtime in Malden. The winter had been long and cold and snowy. Some of the snow had melted, seeped under the roads, and frozen again. When water freezes, it expands, and in the weak places in the asphalt, the newly frozen ice pushes up on the road, cracking it.

Now that it was spring and the ice had melted, the weak places in the roads were being pounded by cars and trucks passing over them. The roads of Malden were riddled with holes. Daniel's parents complained about them when they drove him to school. If they weren't careful, the potholes would damage their tires.

Daniel and Ryan thought about how to help. They decided it would be useful if residents had a way to report the location of potholes to the Malden public works department.

Together, Daniel and Ryan designed and developed their app. Here's how it worked: a user could pull over when they found a pothole, take a picture of it, identify the location, and send the information to the department of public works. When the department got a pothole notification, they could send a team to fix it.

Daniel and Ryan worked on a prototype, a simple version of an app that demonstrates the general concept of how the finished app will work. Then they presented their app at a school showcase. Their teachers and fellow students were impressed.

Daniel's parents weren't the only ones who were bothered by the potholes. When the mayor of Malden heard about the prototype, he wanted to know more! He even invited Daniel and Ryan to his office so they could present the idea to him and the head of the public works department in person.

Daniel (left) and Ryan (center) show their app to the mayor of Malden.

CHAPTER 5

Find the Gold

Now it's time to use some of the cool features of mobile phones and tablets to make a game app! In this maze game, FindTheGold, the user tilts their device to move a ball through the maze. If the ball touches a wall, it returns to the start. If the ball reaches the pot of gold without touching a wall, the game is won.

Import the Template

For this app, you'll use a template project that has all the components already added and most of them placed in the Designer. Go to http://appinventor.mit.edu/assets /files/book/FindTheGold_template.aia and download the file to your computer. The downloaded file will be named FindTheGold_template.aia. In App Inventor, click on the Projects menu and select the downloaded FindTheGold _template.aia file to import.

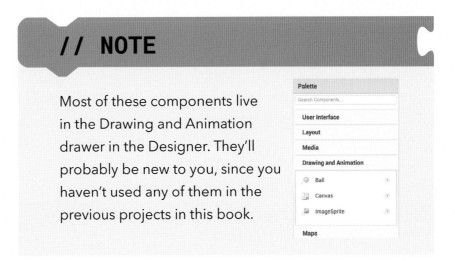
Here are the components that will be included:

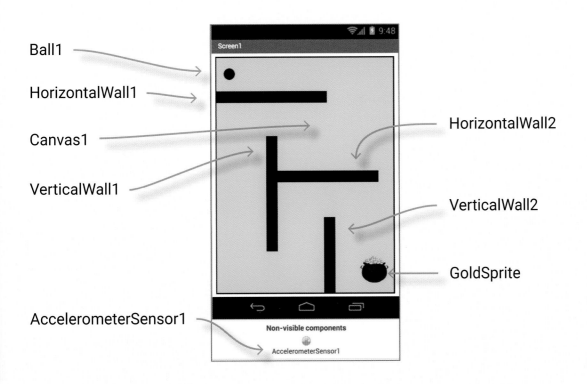

Ball1

HorizontalWall1

Canvas1

VerticalWall1

HorizontalWall2

VerticalWall2

GoldSprite

AccelerometerSensor1

If you look at the picture of the app, you can see the **Ball1** component in the upper-left corner. That's the ball the user will move through the maze. Each of the black walls on the screen is an **ImageSprite** component, made of a simple black rectangle. The pot of gold in the bottom right is called the **GoldSprite**—it's also an **ImageSprite** component.

Balls and **ImageSprite**s are very similar; they can both be animated to change sizes, bounce off the edges of the screen, and fly around in any direction. The main difference between them is that a **Ball** component is always a simple round shape, but an **ImageSprite** can be any shape. Using its Image property, you can set an **ImageSprite** to any picture you upload into the app.

The **Canvas** component is the blank area, or background, of your game. **ImageSprite**s and **Ball**s can only be placed on a **Canvas**.

For FindTheGold, the **Canvas** component covers the entire background area of the app. It's been placed on **Screen1**, and its Width and Height have been set to Fill parent so it takes up the whole screen.

Height

Fill parent...

Width

Fill parent...

106

Placing and Moving ImageSprites and Balls

You can set the position of **ImageSprite**s and **Ball**s on the **Canvas** by their X, Y coordinates. The X is the horizontal position, and the Y is the vertical position on the **Canvas**.

The point (0, 0) is at the top left corner of the screen. X increases as a component moves to the right on the screen. Y increases as it moves down the screen. You may have learned it a little differently in math class, but this is the standard coordinate system used in programming to place and move objects around on a screen.

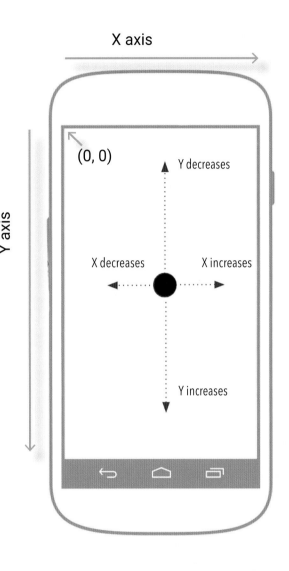

Just as with other components, you can set properties for **ImageSprite**s and **Ball**s in the Designer.

You can also change properties for these components in code blocks.

ImageSprite Properties:

Ball Properties:

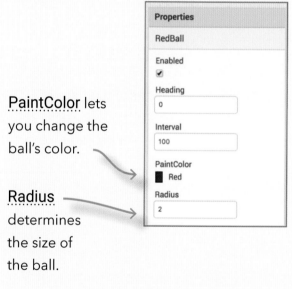

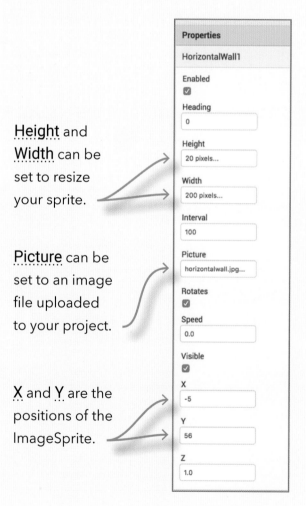

<u>Height</u> and <u>Width</u> can be set to resize your sprite.

<u>Picture</u> can be set to an image file uploaded to your project.

<u>X</u> and <u>Y</u> are the positions of the ImageSprite.

<u>PaintColor</u> lets you change the ball's color.

<u>Radius</u> determines the size of the ball.

Screen Resolution

When you look at the screen of your mobile device, what you're seeing is thousands of little dots of color. These dots are called **pixels**. The more pixels you have, the crisper and more detailed the images look on your screen. The number of pixels on a screen is also called the **resolution** of the screen. More pixels mean a higher resolution.

The resolution of a device also depends on its size. For example, smartphones are often smaller than tablets, so smartphones typically have a lower resolution. As an app developer, you have to plan for different resolutions because you don't know what device your user has.

1) Go into MIT App Inventor and choose Tablet from the drop-down menu above the phone in the Designer. See how all the walls of the maze look like they're pushed toward the upper left? That's because the resolution is higher on the tablet, so the walls appear smaller on the screen. Switch back to the phone display for now.

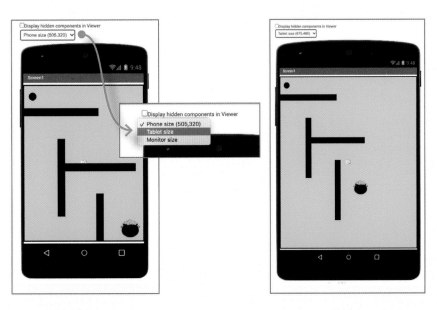

Phone   Tablet

Your app should look good on all devices—small phones, large tablets, devices with high resolution, and devices with low resolution. That's why you'll need to adjust the size and position of the **Ball** and **ImageSprite**s in your app for different-sized screens.

One good way to make sure the size and position of the visual parts of your app work on different resolutions is to use percentages. Instead of setting the X and Y positions of an **ImageSprite** to a particular place on the screen, which might shift if your user is on a device with a different resolution, you can use a percentage of the width and height of the screen or canvas. That way, an **ImageSprite** will be placed in the same spot on the screen regardless of the resolution.

Position the Maze Walls and the GoldSprite

2) Open the Blocks Editor to look at the code blocks in the template. The FindTheGold template includes a procedure called **SetUpMaze** that uses percentages of the canvas size to place the wall **ImageSprite**s and the **GoldSprite**. That way, if the **Canvas** (or screen) is larger, the size and placement of the sprites will look the same.

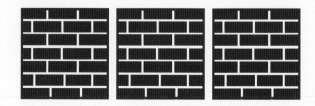

For example, look at the code for **HorizontalWall1**, outlined below in orange. The X position is 0, or against the left edge of **Canvas1**. That will stay the same no matter the screen size. Now look at the Y position. It's set to **Canvas1. Height × 0.2**, which means 20 percent of the Height of **Canvas1**, or one-fifth of the way down from the top. The Width is set to **Canvas1.Width × 0.6**, or 60 percent of the Width of **Canvas1**—a little more than halfway across. This means that regardless of the resolution of the user's device, the wall is still going to be about a fifth of the way down and a little more than halfway across the screen.

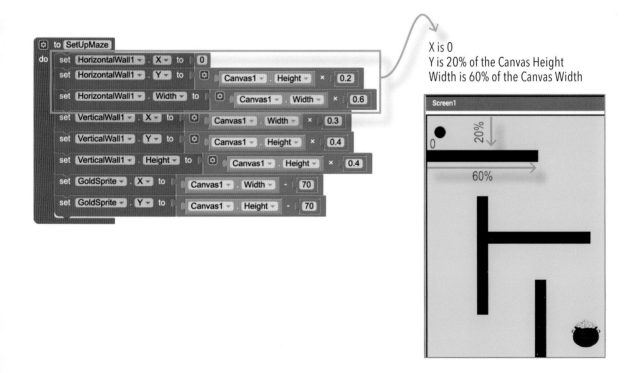

X is 0
Y is 20% of the Canvas Height
Width is 60% of the Canvas Width

Look carefully at the code blocks for **VerticalWall1** to see how that **ImageSprite** is placed and sized.

You want the pot of gold to appear in the bottom right corner of the canvas. If you set its X̲ and Y̲ coordinates to **Canvas1.Width − 70** and **Canvas1.Height − 70**, that means it is 70 pixels to the left and up from the bottom right of the **Canvas**, which will place it in the corner. You don't need to use percentages here because 70 pixels isn't that many, so the pot of gold will be close to the corner regardless of the resolution of the device.

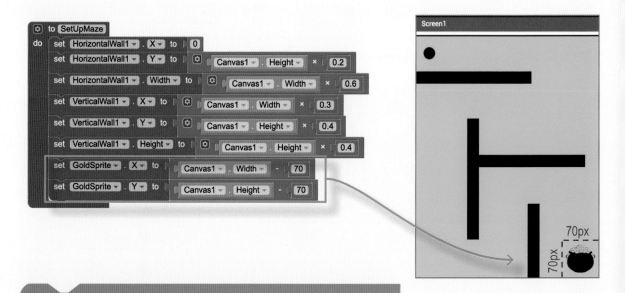

// NOTE

The X and Y coordinates for an **ImageSprite** determine where the upper-left corner of the image will be.

3) You'll need to add the code blocks to set the position and size of the other two walls—**HorizontalWall2** and **VerticalWall2**. The code blocks you need will be similar to the blocks that are already in the procedure, so you might want to duplicate some of the blocks you already have and change the parts. For example, duplicate **set VerticalWall1.X** and then, using the drop-down, change **VerticalWall1** to **HorizontalWall2**.

4) Leave the rest of that block the same. **VerticalWall1** and **HorizontalWall2** should both have the same X position, so they will touch.

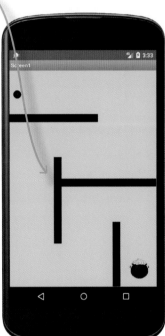

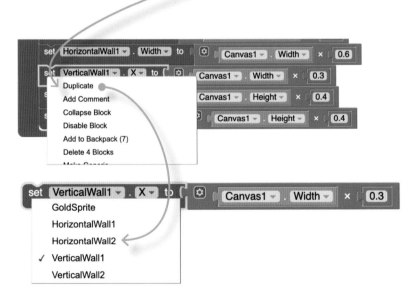

5) Now duplicate **set VerticalWall1.Y** and change **VerticalWall1** to **HorizontalWall2**, then change 0.4 to 0.5 to move the wall down a bit.

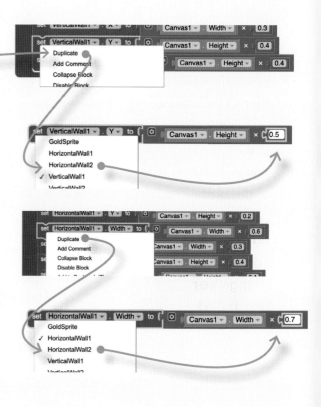

6) Next you'll duplicate **set HorizontalWall1.Width**, change **HorizontalWall1** to **HorizontalWall2**, and change 0.6 to 0.7.

   This will make **HorizontalWall2** a bit wider across than **HorizontalWall1**.

7) Do the same to set the X, Y, and Height for **VerticalWall2**. Copy existing blocks and change the values by using the drop-down menus and typing in the numbers. The result should look like this:

8) Snap all the copied blocks in under the existing ones in the **SetUpMaze** procedure.

Call the Procedure

Now that the procedure is complete, it's ready to be called from someplace else in the app. You want the maze to appear as soon as the app is opened, so it makes sense to call the procedure immediately. The **when Screen1.Initialize** event is the one that happens when an app first opens, so that's where you'll **call SetUpMaze**.

9) Click on **Screen1** in the Blocks palette and drag out a **when Screen1. Initialize** block. Then drag a **call SetUpMaze** block from the Procedures drawer and snap it into **when Screen1.Initialize**.

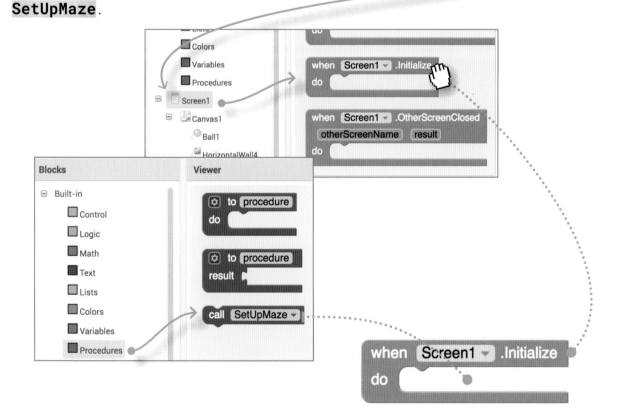

Test and Adjust Your Maze

10) Now is a good time to test the app so you can see how well the maze fits on your device's screen. Connect to the MIT AI2 Companion app on your device and see how it looks!

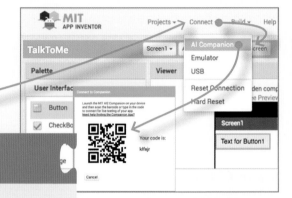

Scan the QR code with MIT AI2 Companion

// NOTE

Because the user needs to tilt their mobile device to move the ball through the maze, you won't be able to test the ball movement using the emulator.

If your maze doesn't look quite right, check that the blocks and percentages are correct. You might also want to change the way the maze looks by adjusting the percentages in the blocks. If you do change any of the blocks, you would normally have to reset and reconnect your device to MIT App Inventor, but here is a tip: once you're connected to the AI2 Companion, if you want to run a code block, you can right-click on the block in App Inventor and select Do It. This runs the block immediately on your mobile device. It's a great way to do some quick testing on the go!

So if you right-click on the **call SetupMaze** block, it will run the blocks in the **SetUpMaze** procedure. If you've shifted parts of the maze around, you'll be able to see those changes.

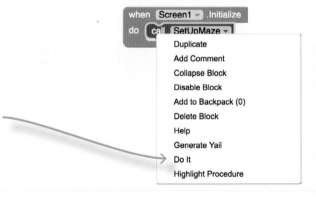

Coding Ball Movements

Now it's time to code the movement of the ball. The ball should move through the maze as the user tilts their screen. On a mobile device, the **AccelerometerSensor** component allows you to measure how much the device is tilted in any direction. You can use that information to update the ball's position.

The **AccelerometerSensor** works by reporting on something called **acceleration**. Acceleration is how quickly a moving object (in this case, the mobile device) changes speed and direction. Anytime the user moves their device, the **AccelerometerSensor** reports that as a change in acceleration to the app. This event is called **AccelerometerSensor1.AccelerationChanged**.

11) Drag out **when AccelerometerSensor1. AccelerationChanged** from the AccelerometerSensor1 drawer.

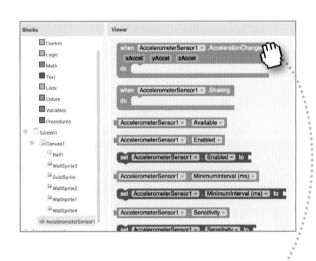

See how there are three parameters in orange that **AccelerationChanged** passes in the event? They're called **xAccel**, **yAccel**, and **zAccel**. These three numbers are the acceleration amounts when the device is moved or tilted.

The screen of a mobile device is flat, but the device itself is three-dimensional. You can tilt the device left or right along the X axis and forward and backward along the Y axis, but you can also move it up or down. This is the third dimension, the Z dimension.

So xAccel reports the amount of acceleration along the X axis, which means how much the device is tilted horizontally, or side to side. yAccel reports the amount of acceleration along the Y axis, which means how much it tilts vertically, or top to bottom. zAccel reports the amount of acceleration along the Z axis, which means how much the device moves in that third dimension, or up and down.

For now, you only need to worry about the X and Y axes, because the ball is only moving in two dimensions across the screen—horizontally and vertically.

You want **Ball1** to move on the screen based on how much the user tilts the mobile device in the X and Y directions— side to side and top to bottom. To do this, you'll use the acceleration of the X and Y positions of the ball.

Move the Ball Side to Side

When a user lifts up the right side of the mobile device, that's considered a positive force in the X direction (horizontally), so the X acceleration is positive, or greater than zero. And when they lift up that right side of the device, **Ball1** should move left on the screen, which means its X position must decrease. So subtracting the positive xAccel from the current X position will make that happen.

Let's give an example. A user lifts the right edge of the mobile device, so the X acceleration is positive. Say the current X position of the ball is 200. If the X acceleration is 7, the X position should move 7 pixels to the left, which means 200 – 7, or 193, for the new X position.

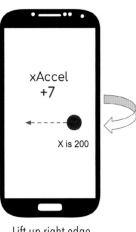

Lift up right edge,
positive X acceleration

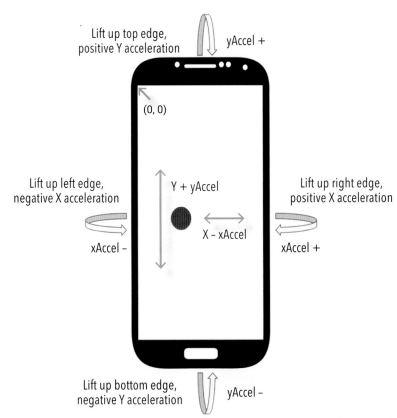

12) Drag out a **set Ball1.X** block from the **Ball1** drawer. Snap it into the **when AccelerometerSensor1. AccelerationChanged** block.

13) From the Math drawer, drag out a ▬ block and snap it to **set Ball1.X**. Remember, you are going to subtract the X acceleration, xAccel, from the current X̲ position, which is called **Ball1.X**.

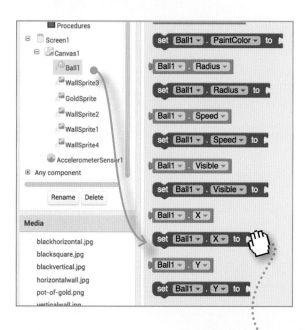

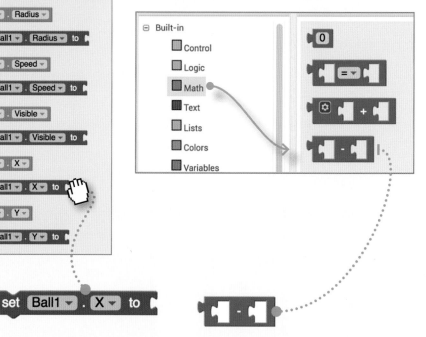

Now you'll need to check to make sure this code will also work when the user lifts up the left edge of their device and xAccel is negative. If the current X position is 100, and if the X acceleration is -7, you want the new X position to be 107, or 7 pixels to the right. Luckily, there is a math property that says that subtracting a negative number is the same as adding the positive of that number. This will work for the ball's movement too. If X is 100, and you subtract -7, the X acceleration, it is the same as adding the opposite of -7. So 100 - (-7) is the same as 100 + 7, or 107.

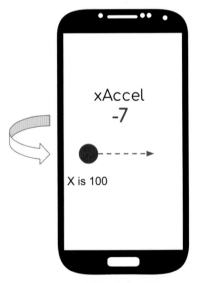

xAccel
-7

X is 100

Lift up left edge,
negative X acceleration

14) Drag out a **Ball1.X** block from the **Ball1** drawer and snap it into the left side of the **–** block.

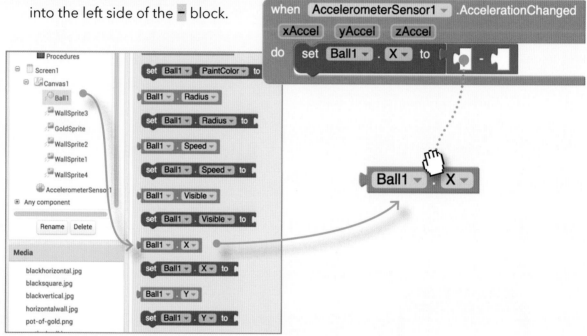

15) Hover over **xAccel** in the **AccelerometerSensor1. AccelerationChanged** block and snap the **get xAccel** block into the right side of the **–** block. This sets the new X position for **Ball1** to whatever the current X position was, minus the X acceleration.

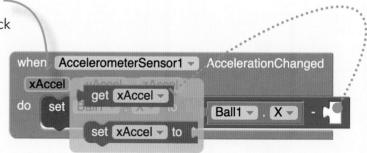

Move the Ball Up and Down

When the user lifts up the mobile device from the top or bottom, that should move **Ball1** up or down vertically, or change the Y position of **Ball1**. Let's look at the acceleration along the Y axis to see how that should work in the code.

If the user lifts up the top of their mobile device, the Y acceleration is positive, or greater than zero, and the ball needs to move down the screen. Therefore, Y should increase.

So it makes sense to increase the Y by adding the positive Y acceleration to the current Y position. For example, if Y is 100 and Y acceleration is positive 11, you add 100 + 11 to get the new Y position, 111.

16) For the Y position, you want to *add* the yAccel to the current Y position, so drag out the appropriate blocks and add them to the **when AccelerometerSensor1. AccelerationChanged** block.

Check that this works when the bottom of the device is lifted. yAccel is negative and **Ball1** should move up on the screen. That means Y needs to decrease. Do you think it will work?

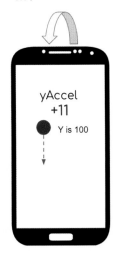

Lift up top edge, positive Y acceleration

yAccel
+11

Y is 100

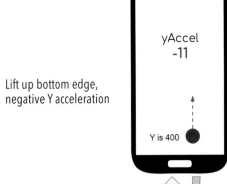

Lift up bottom edge, negative Y acceleration

yAccel
-11

Y is 400

17) This would be a good time to test your app! Connect your project to the MIT AI2 Companion on your mobile device (if it's not already connected). Try tilting your device in different directions. The ball should move based on how you tilt your device. Does it work in all directions?

See how the ball doesn't react when it touches a maze wall or the pot of gold? That's because you haven't yet coded those parts of the app. Let's do that now!

// NOTE

Remember, if you're using the emulator, you won't be able to test your app because the emulator does not have an accelerometer.

Collision Detection

The goal of the maze game is to get the ball to the pot of gold without touching any of the walls. If the ball touches a wall, it should return to the start. If it reaches the pot of gold, the game is won. There is an event block for **Ball** and **ImageSprite** components, called `CollidedWith`, that's triggered when the component touches any other **Ball** or **ImageSprite** in the app.

18) Drag out one of these blocks for **Ball1**.

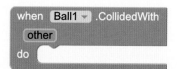

See the orange parameter for this block, called `other`? This other is whatever **Ball1** has collided with. For this app, you want to see whether it was a wall or the **GoldSprite** that **Ball1** hit, so you can either send **Ball1** back to the start or tell the user they've reached the pot of gold!

Depending on the situation, one of two different things needs to happen. If **Ball1** hits a wall, it should go back to the start. If **Ball1** hits the gold, the user has won the game. You need to test what **Ball1** is colliding with by using an **if** block.

if blocks are called **conditional** blocks because they test whether a condition is true or not. Because there is only one **GoldSprite** but there are four wall **ImageSprites**, it will be easier to test for collision with the **GoldSprite**.

If **Ball1** and **GoldSprite** collide, that means the user has made it through the maze and reached their goal. You want to check if that *other* thing that has collided with **Ball1** is the **GoldSprite**. So you want to test if other = GoldSprite.

19) Drag out an **if** block from the Control drawer of the Palette panel.

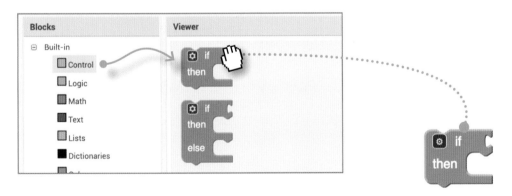

20) To test if two things are equal, you can drag an **=** block from the Logic drawer. Snap it to the **if** block.

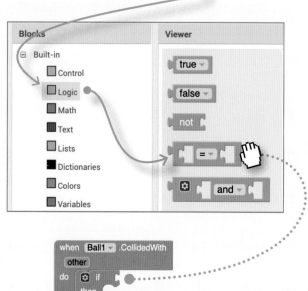

21) Hover over **other** and snap **get other** into the left side of the **=** block and snap **GoldSprite** into the right side. You can find the **GoldSprite** block way at the bottom of the list of blocks for the **GoldSprite** component.

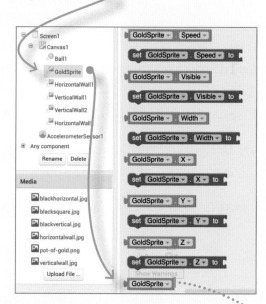

Your **when Ball1.CollidedWith** block should now look like this:

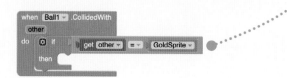

The next thing to code is what should go into the **then** slot of the **if** block. If **Ball1** collides with the **GoldSprite**, you want to stop **Ball1** from moving, because the user has reached their goal. **Ball1** moves when the **AccelerometerSensor1. AccelerationChanged** event happens, so you want to stop that event from running once **Ball1** touches the **GoldSprite**. You'll do that by turning off the **Accelerometer** so it stops checking for any acceleration changes.

22) From the **AccelerometerSensor1** drawer, drag out a **set AccelerometerSensor1. Enabled** block. Snap it into the **then** slot of the **if** block. Whatever blocks appear in the **then** slot are run only if the condition is true. So **AccelerometerSensor1** will stop running only if **Ball1** collides with **GoldSprite**.

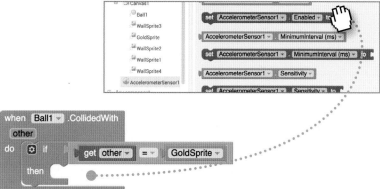

The Enabled property is true if the **AccelerometerSensor** is "on." To turn the component off, you set the Enabled property to **false**. Then it's disabled, and it will stop checking for any changes.

23) From the Logic drawer, drag out a **false** block and snap it into **set AccelerometerSensor1. Enabled**.

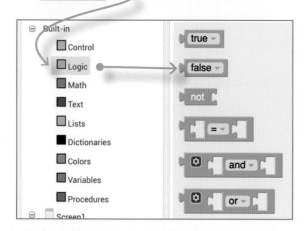

That will stop the **AccelerometerSensor** from sensing tilts, which will stop **Ball1** from moving.

24) Now, if **Ball1** hits any of the four walls, you want it to move back to the starting position. In fact, you want **Ball1** to move back to the start in either case—whether it's a wall it has collided with or the **GoldSprite**. You can use the **call Ball1.MoveTo** block for this. The starting position for **Ball1** is (10, 10). Place this block below the **if** block so that the **call Ball1.MoveTo** block runs in either case—when **Ball1** hits a wall or the **GoldSprite**.

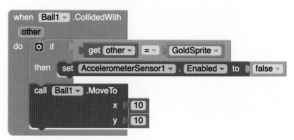

25) Test the app to see how well it works! Does **Ball1** jump back to the start whenever it touches a wall? Can you reach the pot of gold? And does **Ball1** stop moving and go back to the start when it touches the gold?

Notify the User

While this version of the game is fun, when the ball reaches the gold, the user can't do anything else because the **AccelerometerSensor** is disabled. It would be nice to let the user know they've reached their goal and ask them if they want to play again. You can do this with a **Notifier** component.

26) The **Notifier** component hasn't been added to the starter project, so switch back to the Designer.

27) Drag in a **Notifier** from the User Interface drawer. It's a non-visible component, so it will appear below the phone in the Viewer panel.

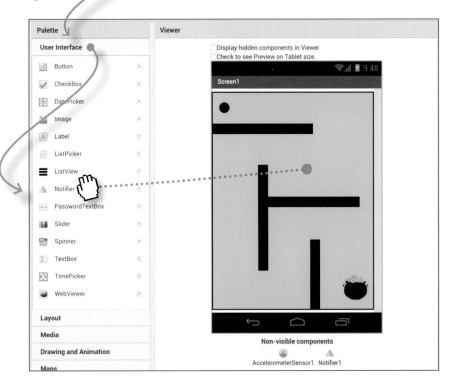

28) Now switch back to the Blocks Editor.

The **Notifier** has a lot of different blocks for sharing information with the user via a dialog box, which will look like a pop-up. There are many options, depending on whether you just want to give the user a message or if you also need them to respond by entering text or clicking a button. For FindTheGold, you want to tell the user they've reached the gold and give them the choice to play again or quit the app.

29) Drag out a **call Notifier1. ShowChooseDialog** block. Snap it into the **then** slot of the **if** block in **when Ball1.CollidedWith**. You only want the notification to appear if **Ball1** has reached the gold, so make sure to add it after the **set AccelerometerSensor1. Enabled** block. That way, the ball stops moving before you notify the user.

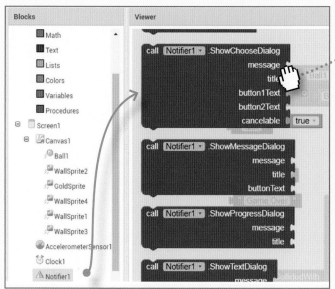

30) There are five slots in the **call Notifier1.ShowChooseDialog** block. The top four slots should be filled in with text blocks for what you want to appear in the dialog box that the user will see. The **message** slot is for the main message. You might add something like **You've reached the gold. Yay!** There is also a slot for **title**, which will appear at the top of the dialog box. This could be something like **Game Over**.

There are also two slots for **button1Text** and **button2Text**. These are for the two buttons that will appear in the dialog box. It makes sense to make these **Play Again** and **Quit**. The **cancelable** slot adds a (Cancel) button if it's set to true. You don't want a (Cancel) button for this app, so change **true** to **false** using the drop-down menu.

The user will see the dialog box and then they'll press one of the two buttons—either (Play Again) or (Quit). The app needs to respond once the user has made their choice. This happens in the **when Notifier1.AfterChoosing** event.

31) Drag one of these blocks out from the **Notifier1** drawer.

32) In this case, you want to do two different things, depending on the user's choice. So you will test using an **if then else** block from the Control drawer.

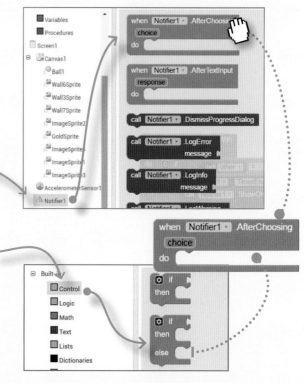

33) Do you remember where you can find the **=** block to test what the choice is?

The Logic drawer!

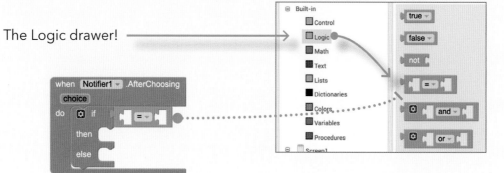

34) You can find the user's button choice in the **choice** parameter included in the **AfterChoosing** block. So hover over **choice** and drag **get choice** into the left side of the **=** block. For the right side, drag in another text block and type in **Quit** to test what will happen if the user chooses to quit the game. Make sure you spell it exactly as you did in the **ShowChooseDialog** block.

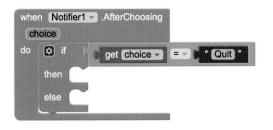

35) If the user chooses to quit the game, you want the app to close. There is a **close application** block in the Control drawer. Snap that into the **then** part of the **if then else** block.

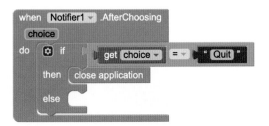

If the user chooses the Play Again button, the code inside the **then** slot of the **if then else** block will not run, because the condition **choice = Quit** is false. So that part of the code is skipped and the program jumps to the **if then else** block. If the user chooses to play again, you want the game to restart, which means the ball needs to move when the user tilts the mobile device. That means you'll need to get the **AccelerometerSensor** running so the ball can move again.

36) Add the blocks to restart the **AccelerometerSensor** by setting its Enabled property to **true**. Snap the blocks into the **else** part of the **if then else** block.

37) That should do it! Try out the app by connecting to the MIT AI2 Companion again. Once you reach the pot of gold, the ball should stop moving and you should see the notification you wrote pop up, asking if you want to quit or play again. Choose (Play Again) and check to see that the ball starts moving when you tilt the device.

If you choose (Quit), you'll get a message that you can't close an application while testing with the MIT AI2 Companion. Don't worry—you'll be able to use the (Quit) button once you've installed the app on your phone or tablet.

You should be very proud! You've just made your first mobile game app!

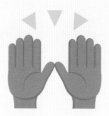

Build the Compiled App

So far, you've made apps and tested them using the MIT AI2 Companion app on your phone or tablet. To run your apps, you've had to open them in App Inventor and connect through the Companion. But what if you want your apps to stay on your phone or tablet so you can open and run them whenever you want?

Here's how you do it. MIT App Inventor project files have an .aia extension at the end of their filenames. For example, with the MyPiano app, you imported the template .aia file into App Inventor. But App Inventor projects can also be packaged into a complete app that can be installed on a mobile device. For Android devices, the file extension for a complete app is ".apk," short for Android package. For iOS apps, the file extension is ".ipa."

Build .apk for Android

To make a complete app, use the Build menu. For Android devices, there are two options to build your complete app—you can get a QR code or save the .apk to your computer. With the QR code option, the code will pop up on your computer screen. Then you can scan it on your mobile device with the MIT AI2 Companion or any other QR code scanner app, and it will download the file to your mobile device. Then you'll follow the instructions that pop up to install the app on your device.

The second option will save a file on your computer with the .apk extension. For the maze game app, the completed app file will be named FindTheGold.apk. You can even email this file to a friend so they can download and install the app on their own device.

Build .ipa for iOS

Building a compiled .ipa file to install on an iOS device is a little more complicated. You can find the full set of instructions here: http://appinv.us/ai-iOS-build.

Extend Your App

Now that you've made your first game, you probably have some great thoughts about how to make it even better! To get you started, here are some ideas for things you could add:

- A countdown timer with a **Clock** component. Now the user has to get the gold in a certain number of seconds.

- Scoring. Give the user points every time they reach the gold!

- Player lives. The user gets only three lives, and every time they touch a wall, they lose a life. The challenge is to reach the gold before they lose all their lives.

- Levels. Now each time the user plays, it's harder to reach the gold! You can even try speeding up the ball's movement with each level so it's more likely to touch a wall.

ARJUN'S STORY

Arjun wrote his first computer program when he was eleven years old. It was a based on a popular Indian television show called *Kaun Banega Crorepati*—a game show similar to *Who Wants to Be a Millionaire?* When Arjun invited his cousins to play the game, the joy of seeing all the events he had programmed unfold perfectly was "unforgettable." He was hooked.

A few months later, Arjun's parents bought their first Android phone, and Arjun discovered MIT App Inventor. Now Arjun could make his own apps.

One afternoon, Arjun's bus was late dropping him off after school because of heavy rains. When he finally got home, he saw that his parents were panicked. They hadn't known where he was or when he'd be returning. The experience gave Arjun an idea: What if there was an app that allowed parents to track their children's location on a school bus? The app could let parents know if their kid was on the bus, share the exact location of the bus on a map, and estimate how long it would take the bus to arrive.

Arjun got to work. At the age of thirteen, he started his own company, LateraLogics, to bring his bus-locator app to market. And the world started to take notice. In

2015, he won MIT App Inventor's App of the Month contest for his Ez School Bus Locator. He also won the National Child Award for Exceptional Achievement, an award given by India's Ministry of Women and Child Development.

Arjun commented on his App Inventor experience: "App Inventor was a great start for me . . . a great tool for experimentally learning." After figuring out how to build apps with App Inventor, Arjun learned other programming languages, which fueled his interest in artificial intelligence, machine learning, and virtual reality. He went on to study computer science and engineering at Lovely Professional University in Phagwara, Punjab, India.

Arjun's company, LateraLogics, continues to grow, always with the mission of creating "innovative solutions that will help make our world a better place."

WHAT IF THERE WAS AN APP THAT ALLOWED PARENTS TO TRACK THEIR CHILDREN'S LOCATION ON A SCHOOL BUS?

CHAPTER 6

Tour Guide

Have you or your parents ever used Google Maps or Waze to find your way somewhere? Apps that use maps can help you get directions, calculate distances and travel times, and even find nearby restaurants and gas stations. In this chapter, you'll make your own tour guide app to show people around your town or city. You'll pick four landmarks or locations that you'd like to show off, and users will be able to click on the markers for each landmark to see pictures and read about them.

You'll also learn how to use the camera component of MIT App Inventor so users can take their own pictures of the landmarks and save them on their phones.

Are you ready to get started?

Do Your Research

Your first step is to do some research. Pick out four landmarks or places in your community that you want to share and gather some information about them. You'll need to write a paragraph to describe each landmark, and you'll also need a picture of each place to use in your app.

Here is a little worksheet that will help you put together the information you need to make your own TourGuide app. For now, fill in the first four columns.

Landmarks Worksheet

Landmark Name	Short Description (one sentence)	Paragraph Description	Image Filename	Latitude	Longitude

Latitude and Longitude

The last two columns are for locating your landmarks on the TourGuide app's map. Remember in the FindTheGold app how you located your **Ball** and **ImageSprite** components using X and Y coordinates on the **Canvas**? For the earth, there is a similar system that's used globally to locate places. Instead of X and Y, locations are identified by their **latitude** and **longitude**. The latitude works like Y and marks a location vertically, and the longitude works like X and marks a location horizontally. They are both measured in degrees.

The equator, which is the line around the middle of the world, is 0 degrees latitude. Latitude increases as you move north of the equator (the North Pole is 90 degrees) and decreases as you move south (the South Pole is -90 degrees).

The prime meridian, which is a vertical line that runs through Greenwich, England, is 0 degrees longitude. Longitude increases as you go east and decreases as you go west.

Every place in the world has its own latitude and longitude. Any location, whether it's on a mountaintop or in the middle of the ocean, can be identified by its latitude and longitude coordinates.

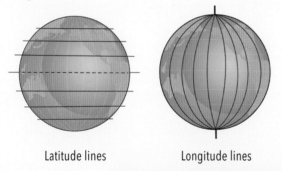

Latitude lines   Longitude lines

// NOTE

Here's a trick for remembering which lines are which: *la*titude lines look like the rungs of a giant *lad*der!

A great website to find out a location's latitude and longitude is http://latlong.net. Open that website and type in your home address. See the latitude and longitude? They will be numbers between –90 and 90 for latitude and –180 and 180 for longitude. You should also see a marker appear on the map at your address.

Using this website, find the latitude and longitude of your four landmarks and add them to your worksheet. The website also takes names of well-known landmarks, so if you don't know the street address, you can just type in names like "Eiffel Tower" or "Washington Monument."

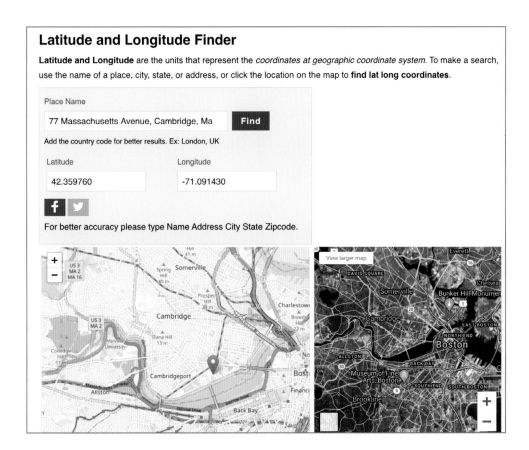

Import the Template

Now that you have the information for your landmarks, you're ready to start building your TourGuide app!

1) Import the starter project for the TourGuide into MIT App Inventor by going to https://appinventor.mit.edu/assets/files/book/TourGuide_template .aia and downloading the file to your computer. The file will be named TourGuide_template.aia.

2) Use a browser on your computer to open App Inventor by going to either http://ai2.appinventor.mit.edu (with your Gmail account) or http://code .appinventor.mit.edu (with return code).

3) Click on the Projects menu, and select Import project (.aia) from my computer …

Select the template file to import. The starter project will automatically open and be added to your projects list in App Inventor.

You'll notice that **Screen1** has just one component so far, the **InstructionLabel**, which gives the user these instructions for the app: "Click on a marker for information. Long-click for more detail on a location." If a user clicks on a marker, they'll see the short description you wrote on your worksheet. If they long-click (or hold down their finger) on a marker, they'll see your paragraph about the landmark and the corresponding picture.

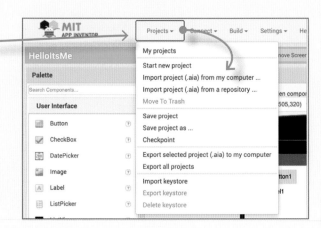

Add the Map Components

4) Open the Maps drawer in the Palette panel, drag out a **Map** component, and drop it below the **InstructionLabel**.

5) Change the <u>Width</u> and <u>Height</u> properties for **Map1** to Fill parent so the map fills all of **Screen1**.

6) In the CenterFromString property, erase what's there and type in your town's latitude and longitude, separated by a comma. (You can find the coordinates for your town or city using http://latlong.net.) Your map should now show the area around your town. The examples here are all landmarks in or near the city of Boston, Massachusetts, in the United States.

7) From the Maps drawer, drag out four **Marker** components and drop them on the map.

8) Change the names of your four **Markers** to the names of the landmarks you put down on your worksheet. Remember, you can't use spaces in component names, so avoid them!

Rename Component	
Old name:	Marker1
New name:	MIT
Cancel	OK

9) For each **Marker**, set the properties based on your worksheet. Set the Description to the one-sentence description you wrote, the Latitude and Longitude to the coordinates you looked up online, and the Title to the name of the landmark (you can include spaces here). And make sure EnableInfobox is checked!

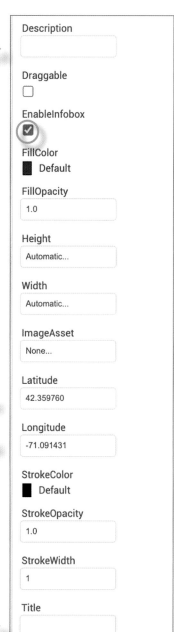

Description

Draggable
☐

EnableInfobox
☑

FillColor
■ Default

FillOpacity
1.0

Height
Automatic...

Width
Automatic...

ImageAsset
None...

Latitude
42.359760

Longitude
-71.091431

StrokeColor
■ Default

StrokeOpacity
1.0

StrokeWidth
1

Title

Now when the app runs and the user clicks on a **Marker**, a gray info box will pop up showing the <u>Title</u> and <u>Description</u> of each place.

10) If all your markers are not visible on the map, drag the map in the Designer to move its center. You can also update the <u>ZoomLevel</u> for **Map1**. If you lose view of your markers, you can zoom out by changing the <u>ZoomLevel</u>.

ZoomLevel

12

// NOTE

The <u>ZoomLevel</u> for a map ranges from 1 to 20, with 1 showing the whole world and 20 zooming in on an address. You can try different numbers between 1 and 20 to get your map zoomed in enough to clearly see all your markers on the screen.

11) You should also check the <u>ShowUser</u> and <u>ShowZoom</u> properties for **Map1**, which will let the user see their own location on the map and zoom in or out.

12) Try testing what you've done so far. Select AI Companion from the Connect menu and click on each of your markers to see if the correct <u>Title</u> and <u>Description</u> appear in the info box.

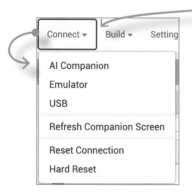

Check Out the LocationScreen

This project has a new feature you haven't seen before: multiple screens. Apps can have more than one screen, which comes in handy when parts of the app look different and need different components and layouts.

For example, in the TourGuide app, **Screen1** shows the map and markers for your landmarks. However, when the user long-clicks on a marker, you'll want the app to display a picture and description of that landmark. It makes sense to use a new screen for the picture and description, since they'll be formatted differently than **Screen1** and the map.

There are three screens in the template, and you can switch between them by clicking on **Screen1**, which is below the navigation menus. The drop-down menu shows you the existing screens. **Screen1** is part of every app and cannot be renamed. But you can name any added screens whatever you want.

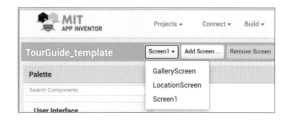

13) Switch to the **LocationScreen**, where you'll add the code to display the pictures and descriptions of the tour landmarks.

14) Take a look at the included components to get an idea of what they'll be used for and how the screen will appear.

Image1

LocationLabel

DescriptionLabel

HorizontalArrangement1

BackButton

TextToSpeech1

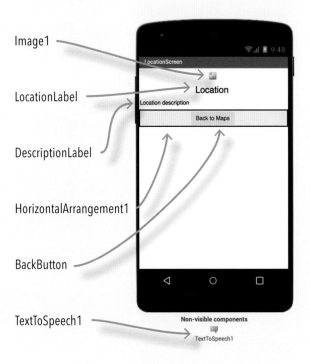

LongClick Events

15) Now that you've seen the layout of the **LocationScreen**, switch back to **Screen1** and open the Blocks Editor.

16) Choose one of your four **Marker** components and drag out a **LongClick** event block for that **Marker**.

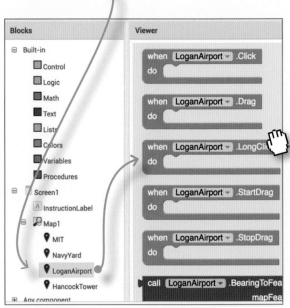

17) From the Control drawer, drag out an **`open another screen with start value`** block and snap it into your **`Marker`**'s **`LongClick`** event block.

18) The **`open another screen with start value`** block has two inputs: **`screenName`** and **`startValue`**. The **`screenName`** will be LocationScreen, so drag out a blank text box and type LocationScreen.

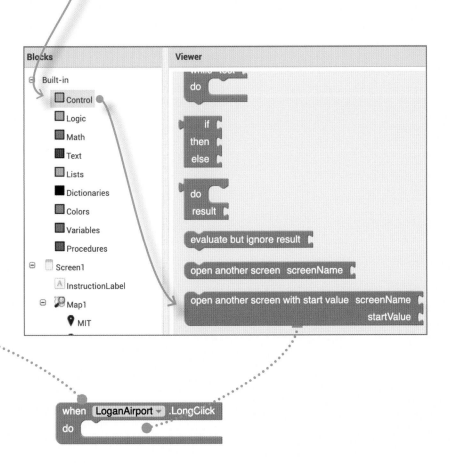

Different screens within an app act almost like separate apps. One screen doesn't automatically know about another screen's components or code blocks. But sometimes screens need to communicate. One way to do that is using the **open another screen with start value** block, which lets you pass information to another screen using **startValue**.

19) What do you need to communicate to the **LocationScreen**? You need to tell the **LocationScreen** which marker information to display. For **startValue**, add another blank text block and type in the name of the corresponding landmark for this **Marker**.

Code the LocationScreen Actions

21) Now you'll switch back to **LocationScreen** to code what happens when that screen is opened in the app.

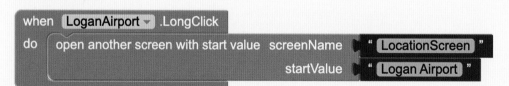

20) Repeat **LongClick** events for your remaining three **Markers**. Make sure to include the corresponding **startValue** for each landmark.

22) Start by uploading images of your four landmarks by clicking on ⌈ Upload File ... ⌉ from the Media tab.

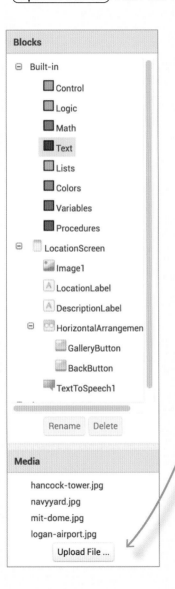

In an app, **variables** are used to store information like game scores, names, and images. They're called variables because they often change, or vary, while the app runs. For example, a variable for a game score will increase as the user gets more points. Giving variables descriptive names, just as you do with components, is good programming practice. It will help you keep track of the information each variable stores.

Your TourGuide app needs access to all the landmark information from your worksheet—the four locations, descriptions, and pictures. You will use variables to store this information. However, instead of using a separate variable for each landmark's location, description, and picture, you'll store all that information in a special type of variable, a **list**. A list is a way to store multiple pieces of information but group them under a single name.

23) Make three variables. Drag out three `initialize global name` blocks from the Variables drawer and change the names to Locations, Descriptions, and Pictures.

The **initialize global** block **initializes**, or sets, the starting value of a variable. It's also the way you set the name of your variable. The word **global** means that the variable is available everywhere within this screen of the app. There are also variables that are **local**, which means they're accessible only in a certain part of an app, like a procedure.

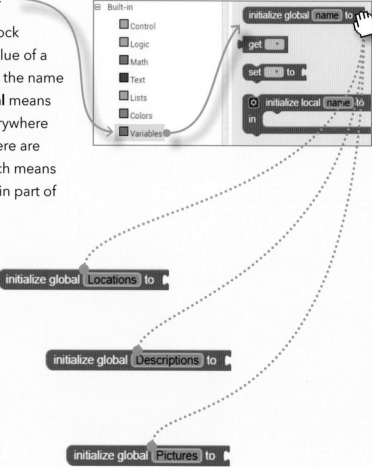

24) From the Lists drawer, drag out three **make a list** blocks and snap them into the **initialize global** blocks.

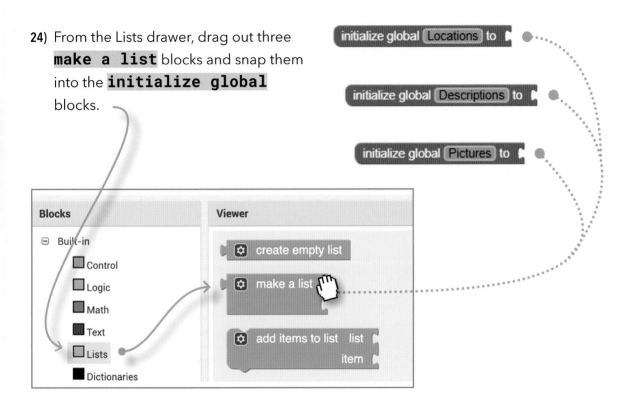

25) For each **make a list** block, click on the blue gear icon to add more items to your list. Add two more items to each **make a list** block so that each block has four empty slots.

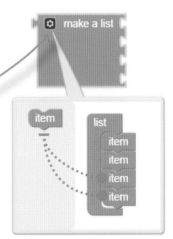

26) In the **Locations** list, snap in four text blocks with the names of your four landmarks. These must *exactly* match the names you used in the **startValues** for the **open another screen with startValue** in **Screen1**.

" MIT "

" Charlestown Navy Yard "

" Logan Airport "

" John Hancock Tower "

initialize global `Locations` to | ⚙ make a list

// NOTE

Why do you have to be so careful about exactly matching your landmark names? Here's the reason. In coding, every letter in the alphabet has a number value, called its ASCII code. For example, the capital letter *A* has the ASCII code 65. The lowercase letter *a* has the ASCII code 97. So even if you made a very small change, like typing in a landmark name with a capital *A* in your **startValue** but then using a lowercase *a* in the **Locations** list, your computer would read their different ASCII codes and see them as two different names. That means your app wouldn't work right.

27) Add four text blocks to the **Descriptions** list, then type the longer landmark descriptions from your worksheet into each one. Make sure the four descriptions are in the same order as your four locations in the list.

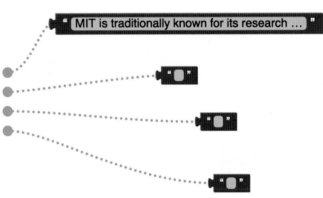

28) To the **Pictures** list, add four text blocks with the image filenames for your landmarks. Remember to type them exactly as they are spelled in your Media panel.

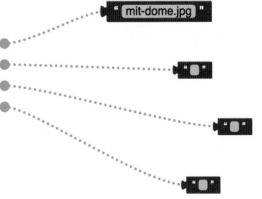

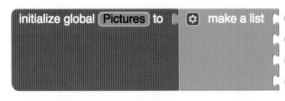

29) Now make a new variable called **locationIndex**. Set its initial value to the Math block **0**.

initialize global (locationIndex) to

// NOTE

Because lists have more than one value, you need something called an **index** to tell your app which item in the list to use. You might think of a list as a filing cabinet. The values are inside the drawers. The index tells you the number of the drawer to open.

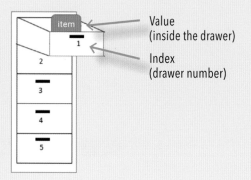

Value
(inside the drawer)

Index
(drawer number)

Get the Corresponding Information for the Landmark

The **locationIndex** will help the app access the right items in each of your three lists: **Locations**, **Descriptions**, and **Pictures**.

Remember how you passed the **startValue** from **Screen1** when opening the **LocationScreen**? Now you'll use that **startValue** to find the correct index for your lists. Because you have the three lists in the same order, once you get the right index, you can use that to pull up the correct location, description, and picture for the chosen landmark. Here is how to do it.

30) Drag out a **set** block from the Variables drawer and choose **global locationIndex** from the drop-down menu.

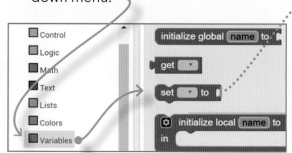

31) From the Lists drawer, drag out an **index in list** block and snap it to **set global locationIndex**.

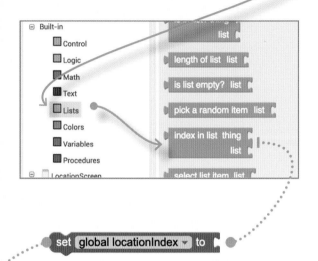

index in list is a powerful block. It looks in a list for a specific thing, and if it finds the thing, it gives you its index. For example, if you look for thing "Logan Airport" in the list of Boston locations below, the **index in list** block will return the number 3, because Logan Airport is the third item in the list. If the thing is not found, it returns 0.

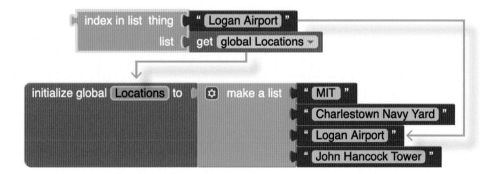

32) For this app, you'll make the list **get global Locations** and the thing **get start value**, which can be found in the Control drawer. So whatever landmark the user clicks on in the map in **Screen1** gets passed to **LocationScreen** as the **startValue**. The **startValue** will be found in the **Locations** list and will give you the correct index for that landmark. And **locationIndex** will help pull the information the app needs to display—location name, description, and picture—from the three lists.

33) You want all this to happen when the screen first opens, so drag out the **when LocationScreen. Initialize** block and add the **set global locationIndex** block to it.

when LocationScreen .Initialize
do set global locationIndex to index in list thing get start value
list get global Locations

34) Now that you have the right index for your landmark, you can display the landmark's information. Set the **LocationLabel.Text** to the item in the **Locations** list that the app will find using **locationIndex**.

35) In **DescriptionLabel**, you'll want to show the landmark's description from the **Descriptions** list. You can save time by duplicating **set LocationLabel.Text** and changing **LocationLabel** to **DescriptionLabel** and **global Locations** to **global Descriptions**.

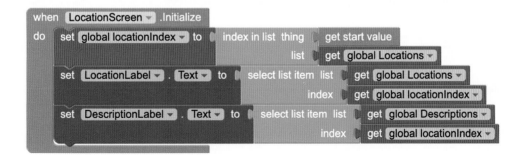

36) Next, set the **Image1.Picture** to the corresponding item in the **Pictures** list.

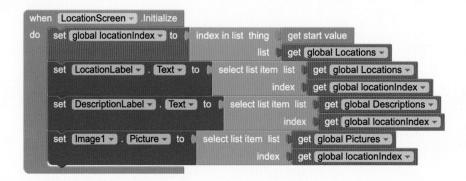

37) To make the app more accessible for users who are blind or have limited vision, add a **call TextToSpeech1.Speak** block to speak the contents of **DescriptionLabel**.

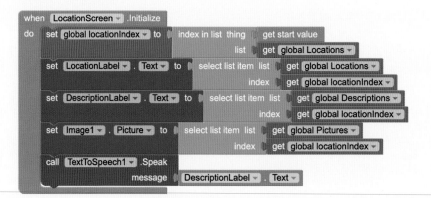

The final thing you need is a way to get back to **Screen1** after the user has learned about the landmark.

38) Add a **when BackButton.Click** event block. From the Control drawer, drag in a **close screen** block and snap it into **when BackButton. Click**.

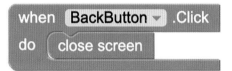

// **NOTE**

When a new screen opens in your app, it appears on top of the screen that opened it. Each new screen you open gets layered on top. So to go back to the original screen, you can use the **close screen** block, which will remove the new screen and uncover the screen below it.

Test Your TourGuide App

It's time to test the app!

39) Go back to **Screen1** so you'll see the map first when the app is loaded. Then connect to your device using the MIT AI2 Companion on your phone or tablet. Try long-clicking on a marker to check that the **LocationScreen** opens and the correct text and picture for that landmark pop up. The app should also speak the description out loud.

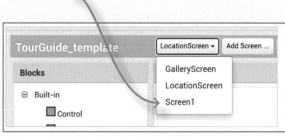

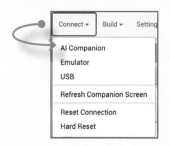

Taking Pictures with the GalleryScreen

So far you've got a working app that lets the user find and learn about different landmarks in your community. What if the user visited those landmarks and decided to take some pictures to remember their trip? For the next part of the app, you'll use a third screen, the **GalleryScreen**, which will let the user take pictures to create a Gallery of their trip.

40) The first step is making sure the user can open the **GalleryScreen**. They'll do that from the **LocationScreen**, so go back to that screen if you don't already have it open, and switch to the Designer.

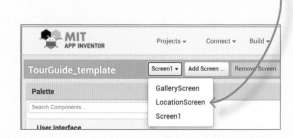

41) Select **GalleryButton** in the Components panel and click on the <u>Visible</u> checkbox to make it visible.

This button will take the user to the **GalleryScreen** to take pictures of the landmarks they see.

42) Switch back to the Blocks Editor and drag out a **when GalleryButton. Click** event block.

43) Drag out an **open another screen** block from the Control drawer and snap it into **when GalleryButton.Click**. This block is simpler than the **open another screen with start value** block you used in **Screen1**. Since you don't need to pass any information to **GalleryScreen**, this block will suffice. The one input you'll need is a text block with **GalleryScreen**.

Code the GalleryScreen

44) Now switch to the **GalleryScreen** to look at its components in the Designer.

This screen is where the user can take pictures of the landmarks they visit. The **Camera** component snaps the picture, which will be displayed in the **Image** component. The **TinyDB** component stores information on the device for use in the app.

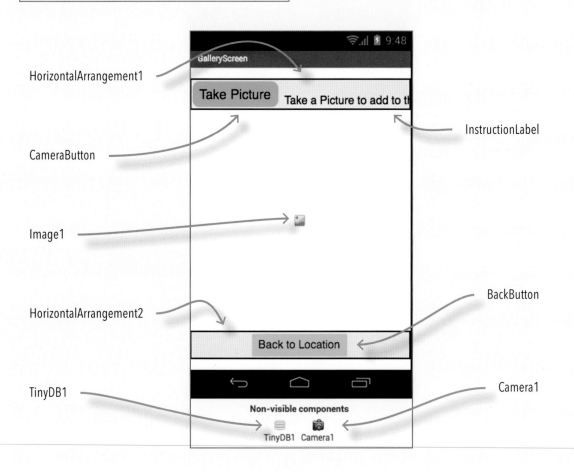

45) Switch to the Blocks Editor to start coding this new feature, and begin by dragging out a **when CameraButton.Click** event block from the **CameraButton** drawer. The user will press the **CameraButton** to open the camera on the device.

46) Click on **Camera1** to see the available blocks. You want to take a picture, so drag out **call Camera1. TakePicture** and snap it into **when CameraButton.Click**.

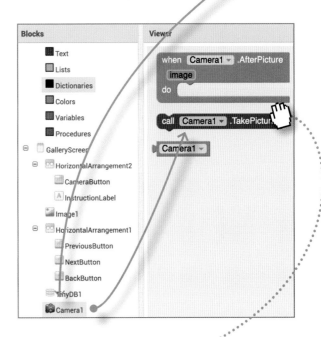

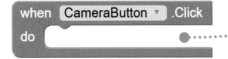

47) The device's camera feature will take over, and after the user takes the picture, the **AfterPicture** event will be triggered. Drag that block out from the **Camera1** drawer.

48) You want to set the image to the picture taken with the camera. So add a **set Image1.Picture** block and attach a **get image** block. That image is a parameter of the event block.

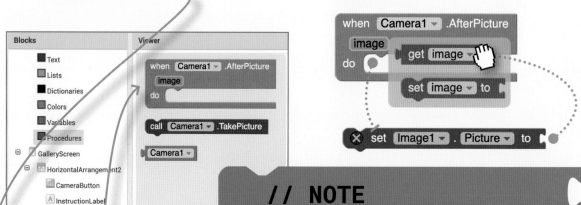

// NOTE

Remember, input parameters are important pieces of information passed to a block. See how the color of parameters is the same as the color of variables? That's because parameters are essentially variables used in a particular way.

49) Test the Camera feature with the MIT AI2 Companion app. Try taking a picture and checking that it shows up in the app.

Store the Image

You want the image to remain, or **persist**, each time you run the app, so if the user closes the app and then opens it again, the last picture they took appears. The **TinyDB** (which stands for "tiny database") component stores information on a device that the app can access again and again.

Apps have memory, which allows them to store and use information when they're running. For example, in the TourGuide app, the `Locations`, `Descriptions`, and `Pictures` lists, along with the `locationIndex`, are all held in the memory of the app. In this app, `locationIndex` changes as the user looks at different landmarks, so the app needs quick access to the current value of `locationIndex` to work properly. However, after the user closes the app, that information is no longer needed, and the user's phone or tablet frees up its memory to do other things, like make a phone call or open a browser.

But sometimes it's useful for the app to remember what happened the last time it ran so the user can pick up where they left off. That is where **TinyDB** comes in. If something is stored in **TinyDB**, it's stored permanently on the device. The app just has to pull it from storage into its memory to use it again. **TinyDB** in the TourGuide app stores the location of the pictures for the Gallery. That way, when the user returns to the app, the pictures will appear again.

50) Click on **TinyDB1** and drag out a **call TinyDB1.StoreValue** block to snap in below **set Image1. Picture**.

You need to give **StoreValue** a **tag** and a **valueToStore**. **TinyDB** uses the **tag**, or name, to find the correct information. The **valueToStore** is the actual information that is stored.

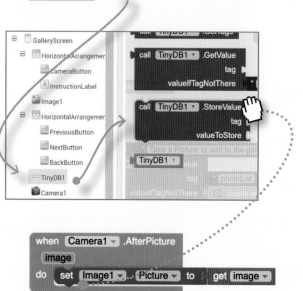

// NOTE

A tag works like a variable name by helping the program locate the information it needs.

51) In this case, you can use **photo** for the **tag**. The **valueToStore** will be the image.

If the user closes the app after taking a picture and then opens the app again, they want to see that picture, the one just stored in **TinyDB**. So your app needs to get the picture and display it when the screen first opens.

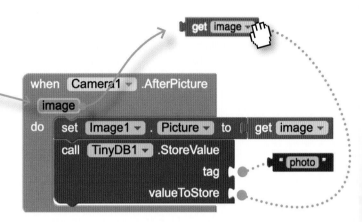

52) Drag out a **when GalleryScreen.Initialize** event block, which will run whenever the screen opens.

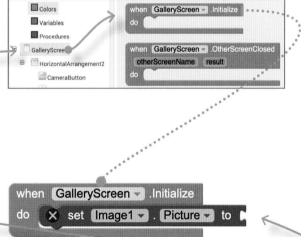

53) Snap in a **set Image1.Picture** block from the **Image1** drawer.

54) Snap a **`call TinyDB1.GetValue`** block to **`set Image1.Picture`**. That block will get the value based on the tag you give it. Make sure it's **photo**, the same tag used to store the value.

But what if the user hasn't taken any pictures yet? The **`valueIfTagNotThere`** slot takes care of that. If nothing has been stored yet in **TinyDB**, the value will be a blank text block so that nothing is displayed for **`Image1`**.

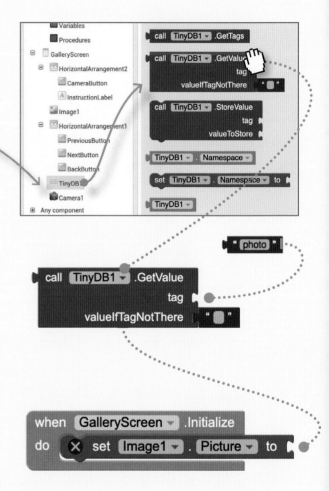

55) Once again, time to test! Remember to go back to **Screen1** before you start testing. Connect to the MIT AI2 Companion. Click on a marker to open the **LocationScreen**, then click on the (Gallery) button to open the **GalleryScreen**. Take a picture. Then close out of the AI2 Companion, go back to **Screen1**, and connect again. Click through to the **GalleryScreen**. You should see the picture you just took!

Add Multiple Images to the Gallery

Wouldn't it be nice to let the user take more than one picture of the different landmarks and store them in the Gallery? You're now going to add a bit more code to do just that.

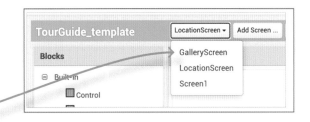

56) Make sure you are in the **GalleryScreen**, then switch to the Designer.

57) In the template are two more invisible buttons. Look in the Components panel for **PreviousButton** and **NextButton**. Check the Visible property for both buttons so they appear next to the **BackButton**. You'll see they show up as Previous Picture and Next Picture.

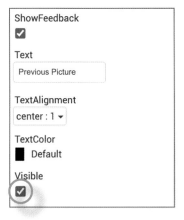

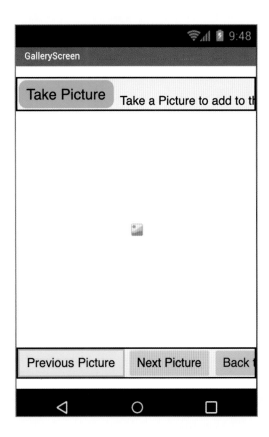

The user can scroll through their pictures with these buttons: (Previous Picture) will take them back, and (Next Picture) will take them forward through their photos.

58) Switch back to the Blocks Editor. Instead of a single photo, you'll let the user add as many photos as they want to the gallery. To help keep track of multiple photos, you'll use a list.

59) Drag out an **initialize global name** block and change the name to **photoList**. Initialize the list to an empty list.

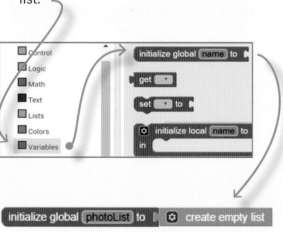

60) When the user takes a picture, the app needs to add the new photo (**image**) to the **photoList**. Open the **Lists** drawer, pull out an **add items to list** block, and snap it in under the **set Image1.Picture** block. Add a **get global photoList** and a **get image** block to the two slots by pulling them from the **Variables** drawer and using the drop-down options.

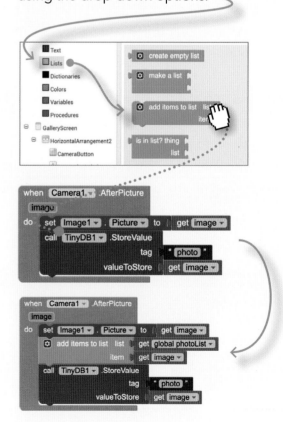

61) You'll use **TinyDB** to store the photos, just as you did before with the single photo. So change the **photo** tag to **photos**. Instead of **image** for the **valueToStore**, change the **valueToStore** to **global photoList** using the drop-down menu.

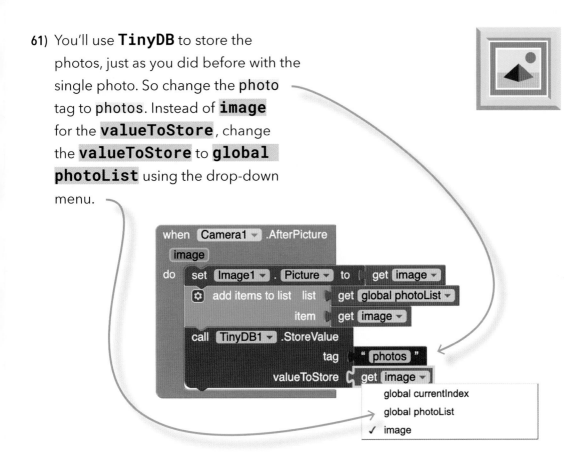

62) Because you have a list of photos, you need a variable to keep track of which photo you are pointing to in the list. This is an index, just like the ones you used in **LocationScreen**. Initialize a new variable and call it **currentIndex**. You can initialize it to **0**.

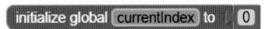

63) **photoList** holds the list of photos, so the app will have to get that list from **TinyDB** when the app opens. Add a **set global photoList** block to **when GalleryScreen. Initialize** and move the **call TinyDB.GetValue** block into it. Change photo to photos for the tag.

64) If the tag is not found, you want **photoList** to still be set to a list. So **valueIfTagNotThere** should not be a blank text block, as it currently is. If there are no photos yet stored in **TinyDB**, you want **photoList** to be set to an empty list. So remove the blank text block for **valueIfTagNotThere** and replace it with **create empty list**.

You want to set **Image1.Picture** to the first photo in the list. But first you want to make sure there's at least one photo in the list. You need to check that the list is *not* empty.

65) Under the **set global PhotoList** block, add an **if** block from the Control drawer, then attach a **not** block from the Logic drawer and an **is list empty?** block from the Lists drawer. This tests if the list is not empty, which means there is at least one photo in it.

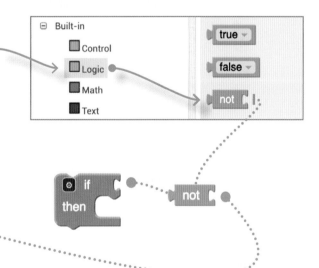

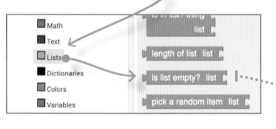

66) Snap a **get global photoList** block to **is list empty?**.

67) If the list is not empty, set
currentIndex to 1, so it points to
the first item in the list.

68) Move the **set Image1.Picture**
block into the **then** part of the **if**
block, because you only want to pull
up the pictures if there is at least one.

Snap a **select list item** block to it,
using **currentIndex** as the index into
the **photoList**.

69) You also want to make sure that when the user takes a new picture, `currentIndex` is updated to point to that picture. Since the most recent photo is the last one in the list, you can use **length of list**, which returns how many items are in a list, to set `currentIndex` correctly.

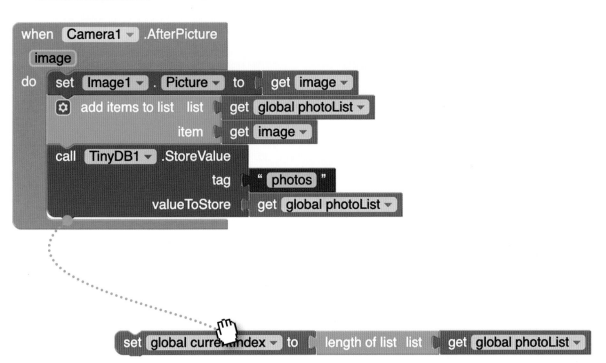

Previous and Next Buttons

Now on to coding the (Previous Picture) and (Next Picture) buttons, starting with the **PreviousButton**. When the user presses (Previous Picture), you want the pointer, **currentIndex**, to move down one photo.

For example, if you have five images in your list, and your **currentIndex** is 2, it points to the second image. Pressing the (Previous Picture) button will ask the app to subtract 1 from **currentIndex**, so **currentIndex** will equal 1 and point to the first image in the list.

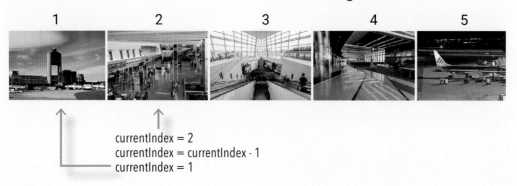

currentIndex = 2
currentIndex = currentIndex - 1
currentIndex = 1

You have to be careful, though. If **currentIndex** is 1, that means **currentIndex** points to the first image in the list.

Subtracting 1 would make **currentIndex** 0, and it would no longer point to an item in the list.

currentIndex = 1
currentIndex = currentIndex - 1
currentIndex = 0

So you have to first check that **currentIndex** is greater than 1 before subtracting 1.

70) Drag out a **when PreviousButton.Click** event block.

71) Add an **if** block from the Control drawer.

72) Drag an **=** block from the Math drawer and snap it to the **if** block. Using the drop-down menu, change **=** to **>**.

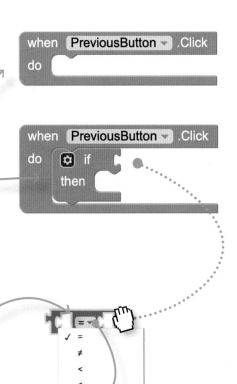

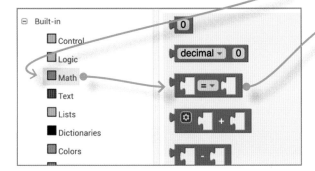

73) Add **`get global currentIndex`** to the left side of the **>** block. Add **1** to the right side of the **>** block.

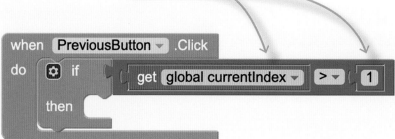

74) Now if **`currentIndex`** is greater than 1, it's okay to subtract 1 from **`currentIndex`**.

75) Once you set **`currentIndex`** to its new value, set **`Image1.Picture`** to the picture at the new index. This will make sure the picture at the updated index is displayed.

Can you code the **`NextButton.Click`** event block? You can copy the blocks and change **`PreviousButton`** to **`NextButton`** to start. Think about what you have to test for with the **`if`** block.

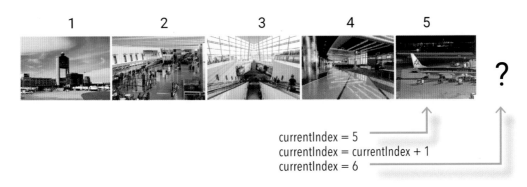

currentIndex = 5
currentIndex = currentIndex + 1
currentIndex = 6

76) Give it a try and see if you can figure it out. If you need some help, the completed blocks are below.

77) The last thing to code is the **BackButton**. This works like your other **when BackButton.Click** event from **LocationScreen**. You just need to close the screen to reveal the screen underneath.

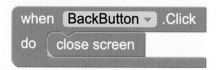

78) Wow! That was a lot! You should have a full-fledged TourGuide app now. Return to **Screen1** and connect to the MIT AI2 Companion to test your app. Go through all the screens, take a few pictures, and see if you can view all the pictures using the Previous Picture and Next Picture buttons.

Extend Your App

There are plenty of ways to add new features to your app! Here are some suggestions:

- Add more markers with different landmarks.

- Let the user type in notes about each landmark in addition to taking pictures.

- Allow the user to delete pictures they don't want to keep.

- Using the **LocationSensor**, set up your app to detect if the user is within ten meters of a landmark and automatically open the **LocationScreen** as they approach it.

What other ideas do you have? Try them out!

HELLO NAVI

When Andres Salas was twelve, he spent his summer learning the layout and the grounds of his new school, Resaca Middle School, in Los Fresnos, Texas. Andres is blind, and he needed time to learn the routes from one classroom to another. Even so, after the school year started, he needed assistance navigating the hallways.

Six of Andres's fellow students—Cassandra Baquero, Grecia Cano, Caitlin Gonzalez, Kayleen Gonzalez, Janessa Leija, and Jacquelyne Garcia Torres—enlisted the help of their teacher, Ms. Bolado, to build an app called Hello Navi to make it easier

THE GIRLS BUILT HELLO NAVI TO GIVE VERBAL INSTRUCTIONS, LIKE "TURN LEFT," AND TO MEASURE THE USER'S STRIDE SO IT COULD KEEP TRACK OF HOW FAR THE USER HAD MOVED.

for Andres and other people who are blind or have limited vision to navigate the school.

The girls talked with Andres to

learn more about what it was like for him to travel from class to class and collected research. They met with his mobility specialist and even walked around the school blindfolded. They went in to school early in the morning, before classes started, to design their app.

The Hello Navi team entered their idea in the Verizon Innovative App Challenge contest, and they were selected as finalists. They were paired with an MIT Master Trainer, who taught them more about MIT App Inventor and helped them complete and publish their app.

The girls built Hello Navi to give verbal instructions, like "turn left," and to measure the user's stride so it could keep track of how far the user had moved. Using Google Indoor Maps and a blueprint they created of their school, they made sure the app had an accurate layout of all the hallways and classrooms.

As Best in Nation winners, the team presented their app at the Technology Student Association conference in Washington, DC. In 2014, the team was recognized by President Barack Obama at the White House Science Fair.

CHAPTER 7

Chat App

So far, you've made several different types of apps—from simple apps that play sounds to games and location-based apps. For your final app in this book, you'll use **CloudDB**, a powerful MIT App Inventor component, to make an app that enables users to communicate between mobile devices. It will be your own personal chat app for talking with friends and family.

Communicating through the Cloud

Have you ever heard someone talk about "the cloud," as in "playing games in the cloud" or "saving pictures in the cloud"? What, exactly, is the cloud? Basically, the cloud is the Internet. If you do something in the cloud, it means that whatever program or app you're using is accessing information or communicating over the Internet, not just running on your personal computer or phone. "In the cloud" makes it seem like there's a big computer hanging up there in the sky, but in reality, the cloud is made up of actual physical servers, which are large computers that store and process information. These computers sit in buildings around the world, not up in the sky. The Internet is made up of hundreds of thousands of servers and networks that connect them using cables, satellites, and Wi-Fi.

CloudDB is short for "cloud database." You might remember using **TinyDB** in the TourGuide app. **TinyDB** lets the user store information from their app on their mobile device. **CloudDB** works very similarly. But instead of storing information on a mobile device, **CloudDB** stores information in the cloud, which means it's stored on a computer server.

When information is stored in **CloudDB**, it also gets passed on to other users of the app. In the picture below, Lena types a message, it gets stored in the chat list in **CloudDB**, and then it gets passed on to Jodi, who is also using the app.

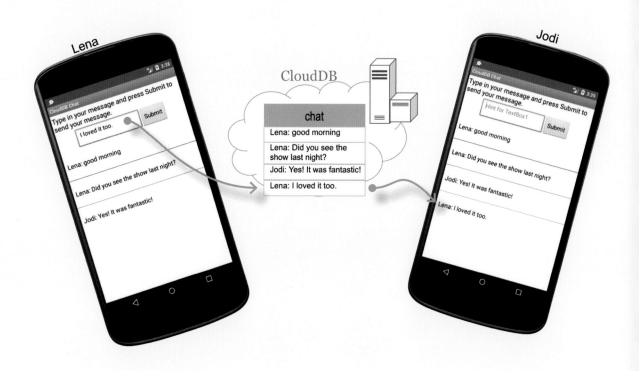

Add the Components

The design of this app is simple. The user types in their name to join the chat. Once they've joined, they can start typing messages. When they press the (Submit) button, their message is added to a chat list that is updated in **CloudDB** and passed on to other users of the app. All messages show up on the app screen, with the name of the user who sent the message at the front.

Let's get started!

1) Open MIT App Inventor and create a new project. Name it **ChatApp**.

2) In the Designer, add the following components and update their properties as shown.

Drawer	Component	Name	Property	Setting
User Interface	**Label**	Label1	Text	Enter your name to join the chat
Layout	**Horizontal-Arrangement**	Horizontal-Arangement1	AlignHorizontal	Center: 3
			Width	Fill Parent
User Interface	**TextBox**	TextBox1		
User Interface	**Button**	SubmitButton	Text	Submit
User Interface	**ListView**	ListView1	BackgroundColor	White
			TextColor	Black
Storage	**CloudDB**	CloudDB1		

Your design should look something like this. Feel free to change the fonts and colors however you'd like.

3) Switch to the Blocks Editor.

Store the Information

When the user first opens the app, **Label1** tells them, "Enter your name to join the chat." The user will type their name in the text box and then press the (Submit) button. Now that they've joined the chat, they can start typing messages to other users. Their name will disappear from the text box, so it needs to be saved somewhere, to be added to their outgoing messages. You'll save it with a variable.

4) Drag out an **initialize global variable** block from the Variables drawer and rename the variable userName. Initialize it to a blank text block.

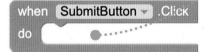

5) Drag out a **when SubmitButton. Click** event block.

6) The user types their name in **TextBox1**. You want to save that in the variable **userName**, so set the variable **userName** to the contents of **TextBox1**.

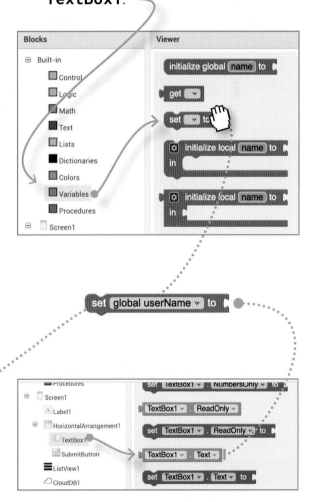

7) Once the user submits their name, you want to update **Label1** to display instructions for the app, something like Type in your message and press Submit to send your message.

```
when  SubmitButton ▾ .Click
do   set  global userName ▾  to  TextBox1 ▾ . Text ▾
     set  Label1 ▾ . Text ▾  to  " Type in your message and press Submit to send yo... "
```

Track User Information

Anytime the user presses Submit from now on, they'll be sending a message instead of entering their name, so the app will need to keep track of which step they are taking.

A good place to keep track of that information is with another variable.

8) Add another **initialize global** block and name this variable joined.

```
initialize global joined to ▸
```

The **joined** variable will store whether or not the user has joined the chat by entering their username. This information is going to be either yes (they've joined) or no (they haven't joined yet). You could store this as a text block, but a more efficient way to do it is with a special type of variable called a **Boolean**. A Boolean variable has one of two values—true or false—and it's used in cases like this.

9) From the Logic drawer, drag out a **false** block as the initial value for **joined**.

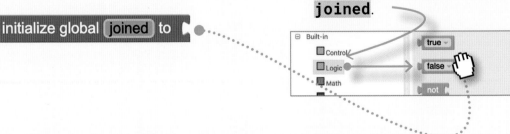

You want to add code to the **when SubmitButton.Click** event block to check whether the user has joined. If the user has *not* joined yet—if joined is false—then save the contents of **TextBox1** in the **userName** variable and change **Label1**.

10) You're testing a condition, so drag out an **if then else** block from the Control drawer and snap it into the **when SubmitButton.Click** block.

11) From the Logic drawer, drag out a **not** block and snap it into the **if** part of the **if then else** block.

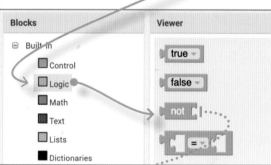

12) From the Variables drawer, drag out a **get** block, and from the drop-down menu, select **global joined** and add it to the **not**.

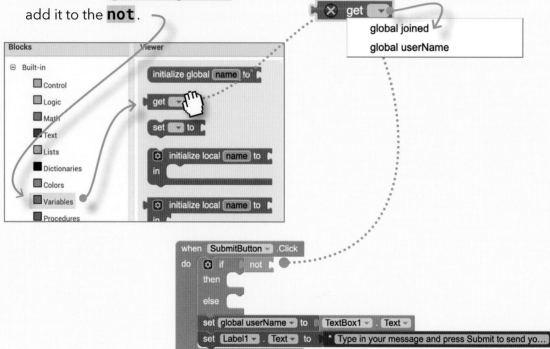

The code **if not get global joined** essentially asks, "Has the user not joined the chat yet?" This is the same as asking, "Is joined false?" Remember that **joined** is a Boolean, so it can be true (if the user has already joined) or false (if the user has not yet joined the conversation).

13) So what do you want to do **if not joined**? Well, you want to do what you've already coded, store the username and change **Label1**, so drag those blocks into the **then** part of the **if then else** block.

```
when  SubmitButton ▾  .Click
do    ⚙ if          not    get global joined ▾
      then   set global userName ▾ to    TextBox1 ▾ . Text ▾
             set  Label1 ▾ . Text ▾  to    " Type in your message and press Submit to send yo... "
      else
```

14) The other thing you need to do is set **joined** to **true**, so the next time the user presses (Submit), the **then** part of the code doesn't run again. It should skip the **then** part of the block and jump to the **else** part of the block.

```
when  SubmitButton ▾  .Click
do    ⚙ if          not    get global joined ▾
      then   set global userName ▾ to    TextBox1 ▾ . Text ▾
             set  Label1 ▾ . Text ▾  to    " Type in your message and press Submit to send yo... "
             set global joined ▾ to    true ▾
      else
```

What code should go in the **else** slot? This is the code that should run when joined is true, which signals that the user is typing a message. You want to store the new message in **CloudDB** so it can be passed on to other users.

Save Messages in the Cloud

A chat is a conversation, with messages traveling back and forth between different users. This means there will be multiple messages, possibly from many different users. If you remember from the TourGuide app, when you want to store multiple pieces of information, it's best to use a list. You'll use a list here too, to store the chat messages in **CloudDB**.

15) Click on **CloudDB1** in the Blocks palette, and drag out a **call CloudDB1.AppendValueToList** block.

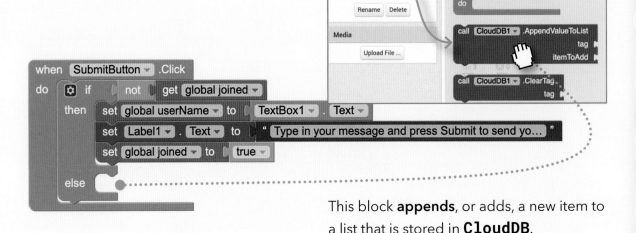

This block **appends**, or adds, a new item to a list that is stored in **CloudDB**.

16) Just as with **TinyDB**, information stored in **CloudDB** has a tag to help identify it. For the chat app, you can simply name the **tag** chat. The **itemToAdd** will be the new message, which is the contents of **TextBox1**. It will be useful to include the author of the message when you're storing it—you can use the **join** block from the Text drawer to include the **userName**. To make it easier to read, add a colon followed by a space (:) between the **userName** and message.

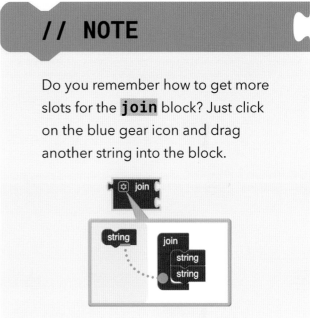

// NOTE

Do you remember how to get more slots for the **join** block? Just click on the blue gear icon and drag another string into the block.

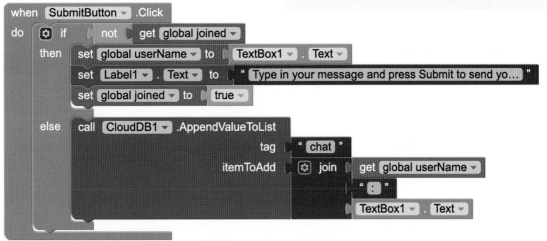

17) After this, you want to clear whatever's in **TextBox1**, so add a block to set it to blank text.

```
when  SubmitButton ▾ .Click
do   ⚙ if       not   get global joined ▾
     then  set global userName ▾ to   TextBox1 ▾ . Text ▾
           set Label1 ▾ . Text ▾ to  " Type in your message and press Submit to send yo... "
           set global joined ▾ to   true ▾

     else  call CloudDB1 ▾ .AppendValueToList
                                    tag  " chat "
                             itemToAdd   ⚙ join   get global userName ▾
                                                  " : "
                                                  TextBox1 ▾ . Text ▾

     set TextBox1 ▾ . Text ▾ to  "  "
```

Check for User Error

When coding, it's useful to think about ways users might use the app incorrectly. For example, what if the user mistakenly presses (Submit) before typing anything in the text box? You don't want them to have a blank username or add blank messages to the chat, so inserting some code to prevent that can make the app more user-friendly.

18) Drag out an **if** block from the Control drawer and test whether **TextBox1** is not empty. Add it to the **when SubmitButton.Click** block and put all the existing code inside that block. Your completed blocks should look like this:

```
when SubmitButton ▾ .Click
do    ⚙ if       not   is empty   TextBox1 ▾ . Text ▾
      then  ⚙ if      not   get global joined ▾
            then  set global userName ▾ to   TextBox1 ▾ . Text ▾
                  set Label1 ▾ . Text ▾ to   " Type in your message and press Submit to send yo… "
                  set global joined ▾ to   true ▾
            else  call CloudDB1 ▾ .AppendValueToList
                              tag   " chat "
                              itemToAdd   ⚙ join   get global userName ▾
                                                    " : "
                                                    TextBox1 ▾ . Text ▾
      set TextBox1 ▾ . Text ▾ to   "     "
```

This new block first checks that there is something in the text box before running through any of the other code. If the text box is empty, it will just skip over the code and do nothing. If there is something in the text box, it's not empty, so the code will run.

Updating Users

Let's say a user joins the conversation and types in a message, which gets stored in **CloudDB1**. Now **CloudDB1** needs to send that information to all users of the app so they get the new message. You can make that happen using an event block for **CloudDB1** called **DataChanged**, which runs whenever any information is stored, changed, or deleted in **CloudDB1**.

19) Drag out a **when CloudDB1. DataChanged** event block.

Notice that **DataChanged** has two parameters, **tag** and **value**. **CloudDB1** passes those two pieces of information to the app. Even though there is only one tag, **chat**, for this app, you might decide to add more when you expand the app. It's good practice to check that you have the correct tag when **CloudDB1** sends information.

20) Drag out an **if** block from the Control drawer and add it to **when CloudDB1.DataChanged**.

21) Using the **=** block from the Logic drawer, test that **tag = chat**, which is the tag you used when adding the new message to the chat list.

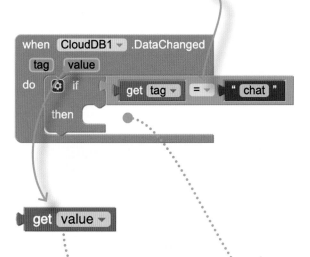

22) Once you know you have the correct tag, you know that the value is the list of chat messages. You'll want to display the list so users can read the updated messages, and you can do that with the **ListView** component. Set the Elements property to **value**, so that the full updated list of chat messages is displayed.

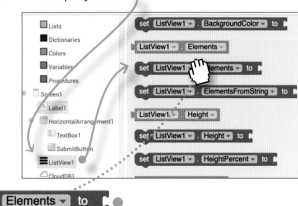

// NOTE

The **ListView** component is for viewing a list. You'll have to tell the **ListView** component which list it should display by setting its Elements property. Once you set Elements to the list you want, that's what will be displayed in the **ListView**.

Update New Users

The **DataChanged** event happens whenever there's a new message and **CloudDB1** sends out the updated chat list. But what happens when a new user opens the app to join a conversation that's already started? They need to be caught up on the previous messages. Remember that when the app starts, the **Screen1. Initialize** event runs. You can use that event to get any messages stored in the chat from **CloudDB1** and display them in the **ListView** component.

23) Drag out a **when Screen1. Initialize** block.

24) From the **CloudDB1** drawer, drag out a **call CloudDB1.GetValue** block. This block asks **CloudDB1** for the current value of a given tag, in this case **chat**. Because the value is a list, if the tag is not found, make sure **CloudDB1** returns an empty list.

Remember that **CloudDB1** is in the cloud, which means the information is stored on a computer server (in this case, a server in Cambridge, Massachusetts!). The app requests the information from **CloudDB1** via the Internet, and **CloudDB1** looks for the tag and then sends the corresponding value back to the app. This doesn't happen immediately, like when you **GetValue** from **TinyDB**, which is on your phone. It could take a few seconds before **CloudDB1** sends the requested information back to the app. Once the app gets the information, the **GotValue** event is triggered.

25) Drag out a **when CloudDB1. GotValue** block.

This event needs to do exactly what the **DataChanged** event did—update **ListView1.Elements** with the current value of the **chat** tag.

26) Find the **DataChanged** block, and right-click on the **if** block inside and duplicate the blocks. Snap the duplicated blocks into **when CloudDB1.GotValue**.

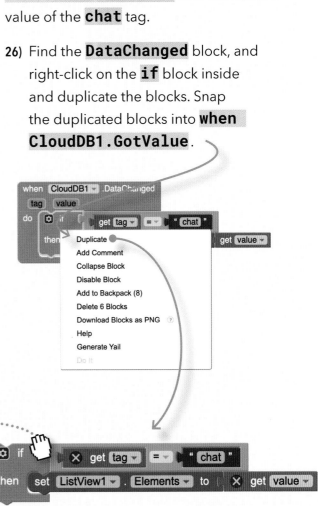

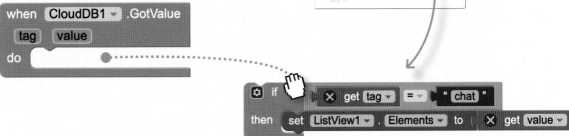

Test Your App

That's it! Now comes the fun part: trying it out! The best way to test this app is to get a friend or family member to load it on their phone so you can send messages to each other through the cloud.

To test the app with multiple devices, you'll need to build the .apk (if you're using an Android device) or .ipa (if you're using an iOS device) and install the completed app instead of using the AI2 Companion in test mode.

If you and your friend are using iOS devices, please refer to page 135 for how to install the .ipa file on your device. If you're using Android devices, follow the next three steps.

27) From the Build menu, select App (provide QR code for .apk).

It will take several seconds to build the .apk, and then a QR code will appear on your computer screen.

28) Scan the QR code with a QR code scanner app on your mobile device. You can also use the AI2 Companion app to scan the QR code. Follow the instructions to download and install the app. If possible, get your friend or family member to do the same on their mobile device.

// NOTE

Your device may not allow apps to be installed from somewhere other than the Google Play Store. If you get a message stating that, go to your device's Settings, and in the Security screen, check the box to enable Install from Unknown Sources. That should do the trick!

29) Notice that this QR code is good for only two hours, so if you want to share your app with friends, go back to the Build menu and choose App (save .apk to my computer). Once MIT App Inventor builds the .apk, the file is saved on your computer. You can then email the .apk to your friends to install on their mobile devices.

Once you and your friends have installed the app, open it and start chatting!

Extend Your App

Congratulations on finishing your chat app! Here are some suggestions for making it even better:

- Add a time stamp to each message using the **Clock** component so users know when each message was sent.

- Reverse the order of the messages so the most recent message appears at the top of the **ListView**.

- Add a button to erase a chat and start over.

- Add multiple chat rooms so users can make smaller group chats within the app.

What else can you think of?

CHINMAYI'S STORY

I have always been extremely interested in computers and coding. When I was in second grade, I started playing with Scratch [another coding language], making games, and publishing them. When I was in fourth grade, my mom introduced me to App Inventor. Immediately, I loved the idea of making stuff that anyone could use, wherever they were. Much to my surprise, it was really easy to get started and to build a functional app. The App Inventor website also had tutorials that I could follow. I decided I wanted to make an app that would actually help people and make a difference.

Just a few months later, I got my chance. Heavy rains, followed by devastating floods, hit several parts of Tamil Nadu in south India, bringing life there to a standstill. Many residents lost their houses and belongings. When I was talking to relatives who lived there, I realized that many people wanted to help the flood victims but had no idea how. So I made an app that showed nearby centers for people to drop off their donations and enabled flood victims to list what they already had and what they still needed.

After finishing my app, I uploaded it to the Google Play Store. When people took notice of my app and congratulated me, I felt really happy and encouraged to make more apps.

The next year, I made an app called PlugTheDrip that notifies you if any of the taps in your house are leaking and helps you find plumbers. This app can help you save water around the house while helping plumbers find more business. I presented this app in the MIT App Inventor Summit 2016 and managed to win second place!

I also made an app called PuffIn to help people suffering from asthma. I was inspired to make this app when I saw my mom suffering from asthma attacks due to the high pollution levels in my city of Bangalore. I installed gas and touch sensors in an inhaler along with an Arduino (a small electronic board with sensors that can be programmed to perform tasks). The Arduino would constantly send information about the pollution levels in the surrounding environment to my app. The app would warn the user if the pollution levels got too high

"I WAS INSPIRED TO MAKE THIS APP WHEN I SAW MY MOM SUFFERING FROM ASTHMA."

so that the user would be prepared with the inhaler when their attack arrived. It would also notify the user when it was time to get a new inhaler. This app was the runner-up in the Technovation Challenge.

Then I decided to make an app to help me wake up on time. I often got up late, and missing my bus was almost a habit. I called my app XSolviturAmbulando. It would ring when it was time to wake up and wouldn't stop until I walked ten steps with it. To snooze the alarm, I would have to solve puzzles. I learned a lot about how to use sensors and other components in App Inventor. I submitted my app to the Google Code to Learn competition and was one of the winners there.

App Inventor is a really fun and engaging way to make helpful apps easily and quickly. It helped me grasp the basic concepts of programming like loops and variables. This helped me a lot with learning other programming languages and has enabled me to comprehend them better.

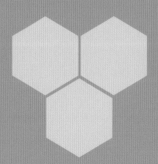

CONCLUSION

Now that you've created six different mobile apps, and hopefully found unique ways to improve your apps by adding new features, you're well on your way to becoming an app inventor!

More Components

Even though you've learned a ton about MIT App Inventor and many of its components, there's still lots more to explore. From the User Interface drawer, you might try some of the other components to see how they work. For example, the **Slider** component lets the user set a number value by moving their thumb along the bar to make the value larger or smaller.

Not sure what a component does? Find the little question mark to the right of each component in the Palette. If you click on the question mark, a pop-up window will appear with an explanation of how the component works.

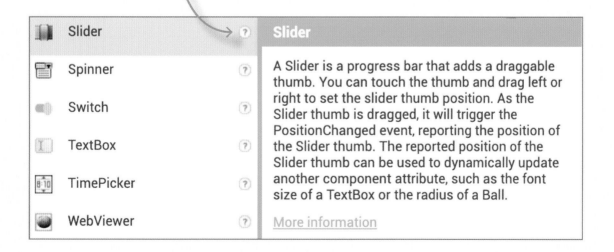

Although you've used a few of the components in some of the other drawers, like Media, Maps, and Sensors, you can see that there are many more to check out.

The Social drawer contains components that use more smartphone features like texting and making phone calls from within an app. The Connectivity drawer lets you connect to other apps on your phone, connect to other devices through Bluetooth, and gather information from the web.

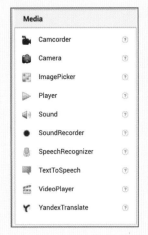

Media

- Camcorder
- Camera
- ImagePicker
- Player
- Sound
- SoundRecorder
- SpeechRecognizer
- TextToSpeech
- VideoPlayer
- YandexTranslate

Maps

- Circle
- FeatureCollection
- LineString
- Map
- Marker
- Navigation
- Polygon
- Rectangle

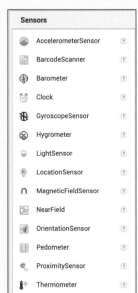

Sensors

- AccelerometerSensor
- BarcodeScanner
- Barometer
- Clock
- GyroscopeSensor
- Hygrometer
- LightSensor
- LocationSensor
- MagneticFieldSensor
- NearField
- OrientationSensor
- Pedometer
- ProximitySensor
- Thermometer

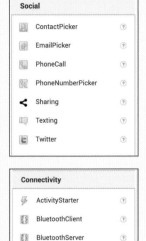

Social

- ContactPicker
- EmailPicker
- PhoneCall
- PhoneNumberPicker
- Sharing
- Texting
- Twitter

Connectivity

- ActivityStarter
- BluetoothClient
- BluetoothServer
- Serial
- Web

Find More Inspiration

There are so many possibilities for apps to make. It's up to you to use your imagination and follow your interests. Remember to bring your passion to whatever you create!

If you are looking for inspiration, you can also check out more resources on the MIT App Inventor website: http://appinventor .mit.edu. You can even go to the Tutorials page in the Resources menu to find tutorials to try.

App Inventor also has a YouTube channel (https://www.youtube.com/c /MITAppInventor123) with many tutorials and presentations.

Another great place for inspiration is the App of the Month collection in the About menu. Every month, people from all around the world submit their apps to be judged by App Inventor staff. Top apps are awarded an App of the Month badge and are posted on the website.

A link to every winner's project is included, so you can open the project yourself to see the design and code blocks. It's a great way to learn from others. Why not submit your own apps to the App of the Month contest? Your awesome app could appear on the website too!

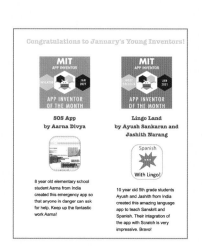

Share with Others

App Inventor also has a Gallery feature so inventors can share their projects.

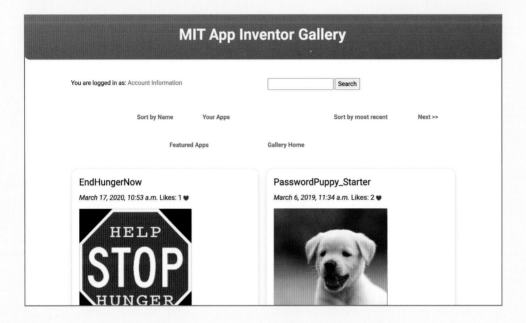

When you make a really cool app that you'd like to share with other app inventors, just click on the (Publish to Gallery) button at the top of the App Inventor interface.

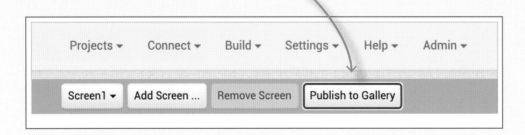

You'll be asked to input a description and picture for your app, and then it will show up in the Gallery. To find the Gallery and see what apps others have contributed, go to your Project page, then click the (Login to Gallery) button.

Another great resource as you start to create more apps with your new App Inventor skills is the community forum (https://community.appinventor.mit.edu), an online platform where app inventors from around the world ask questions, share ideas, and learn from one another. An active group of "power users" is very friendly and ready to help answer any technical questions you may have.

With all that you've accomplished by making the apps in this book, along with these additional resources, you've got everything you need to make some incredible apps. The App Inventor team looks forward to seeing your apps in the Gallery, in the App of the Month contest, and even on the Play Store and App Store. *Happy* inventing!

ACKNOWLEDGMENTS

This book has been a long time in coming, and we have several people to thank for their part in making it happen. First, of course, is MIT professor Hal Abelson, who had the vision for App Inventor back in 2007, when on sabbatical at Google. Hal, along with Google engineers Mark Friedman, Liz Looney, Ellen Spertus, Debby Wallach, and Karen Parker, and with the encouragement of Maggie Johnson and Alfred Spector, created the App Inventor platform, which has been used by millions of people worldwide, building nearly 60 million mobile apps as of this writing.

The apps in this book were born out of the CoolThink@JC project, a collaboration between MIT and the Education University of Hong Kong. We are thankful for the partnership and work of our colleagues in Hong Kong, who helped us create the CoolThink curriculum, taught to thousands of students in Hong Kong. We are also grateful to the Hong Kong Jockey Club Charities Trust for funding this tremendous project.

The translation app is part of a series of app-building guides we developed in partnership with YR Media of Oakland, California. Thanks go to the team at YR Media for their creativity and inspiration in helping us develop meaningful app ideas for young people.

We also want to acknowledge the MIT App Inventor staff for their commitment to the mission of App Inventor. Thanks to members of the development team, past and present, including Andrew McKinney, Jeff Schiller, Evan Patton, Susan Lane, and Li Li, for their commitment to improving App Inventor to make it the easy-to-use and helpful tool it is.

Thanks to the education team members who contributed over the past few years to the CoolThink curriculum by managing, writing, testing, and revising. Thank you, Josh Sheldon, Natalie Lao, Mike Tissenbaum, Farzeen Harunani, Mark Sherman, David Tseng, and Ting-Chia Hsu, for your input and assistance in building the curriculum that was the basis for this book.

Thank you also to App Inventor administrative staff, including Marisol Diaz, Drew Nichols, and Cindy Rosenthal, for making the project tick along and helping us out in myriad ways. And thanks to MIT student Jimin Lee for meticulously following the book's instructions to catch any errors.

We also would like to thank Candlewick Press for taking on this project with us. In particular, thanks to our editor, Olivia Swomley, who guided us through writing this book, pushed us to put technical information into understandable language, and taught us a lot about publishing. And thank you to Hai-Wen Lin for their amazing design work, which brought the book to life.

Finally, thanks go to our families. From Selim, thanks to my wife, Jingyan Zhao, and my son, Alan Tezel, for their inspiration and support. From Karen, thanks to my partner, Debbie, for always believing in me and pushing me to be the best I can be.

Bibliography

Bender, Kelli. "Texas Middle Schoolers Win National Contest for App Inspired by Their Blind Classmate." People.com, March 25, 2014. https://people.com/human-interest/verizon-innovative-app-challenge-winners-share-the-story-of-hello-navi/.

Colorado Pavement Solutions. "How Do Potholes Form?" December 18, 2019. https://copavementsolutions.com/how-do-potholes-form/.

Cox, Heather Cathleen. "Middle School App Developers Shine National Spotlight on Los Fresnos." *San Benito News*, July 1, 2014. https://www.sbnewspaper.com/2014/07/01/middle-school-app-developers-shine-national-spotlight-on-los-fresnos/.

Feliú-Mójer, Mónica I. "Middle Schoolers Develop App to Help Visually Impaired." *Voices* (blog). *Scientific American*, October 15, 2014. https://blogs.scientificamerican.com/voices/middle-schoolers-develop-app-to-help-visually-impaired/.

Laneri, Raquel. "A Group of Tween Girls Use a Competition to Launch Hello Navi, an App Designed to Help Their Blind Classmate." Metro.us, October 30, 2015. https://www.metro.us/a-group-of-tween-girls-use-a-competition-to-launch-hello-navi-an-appdesigned-to-help-their-blind-classmate/.

Moreland, Chip. "How Do You Get Girls Involved in Global Technology? Just Ask." Peace Corps, December 8, 2014. https://www.peacecorps.gov/stories/how-do-you-get-girls-involved-in-global-technology-just-ask/.

NYU Langone Health. "Types of Hepatitis." Accessed July 2, 2021. https://nyulangone.org /conditions/hepatitis-a-b-c/types.

"Obama Unleashes His Inner Geek (Again) at White House Science Fair." NBCNews.com, May 27, 2014. https://www.nbcnews.com/science/science-news/obama-unleashes -his-inner-geek-again-white-house-science-fair-n115451.

Reader, Ruth. "Code Girl Documentary Perfectly Sums Up Why More Girls Don't Code." VentureBeat, November 4, 2015. https://venturebeat.com/2015/11/04/code-girl -documentary-perfectly-sums-up-why-more-girls-dont-code/.

"Technovation Ștefănești Pitch Video." Aqua Mea, May 1, 2014. YouTube video, 4:03. https://youtu.be/1cnLiSySizw.

United Nations Development Programme: Moldova. "Clean Water and Sanitation." Accessed July 2, 2021. https://www.md.undp.org/content/moldova/en/home /sustainable-development-goals/goal-6-clean-water-and-sanitation.html.

"World's First FREE School Bus Tracking Mobile Phone App Solution for Schools." Ez School Bus Locator. Accessed July 2, 2021. https://ezschoolbuslocator.mystrikingly.com/.

INDEX

Index (cont.)

PHOTO CREDITS